SINCE
YOU
ASK
ME

By Ann Landers

PRENTICE-HALL, INC. • ENGLEWOOD CLIFFS, N.J. 07632

ISBN 0-13-810531-6 {A REWARD BOOK : PBK.}

Library of Congress Catalog Card Number: 61-15070

First printing ...... August, 1961
Second printing ..... August, 1961
Third printing .... September, 1961

81035-T

For Margo

Contents

About Ann Landers

Courage and fortitude are words seldom used and virtues rarely practiced in a world of anxieties, indifferences, and false securities. And yet—

Since You Ask Me could well have been called *The Courage of Ann Landers.* Because Ann Landers has courage, and at a time when courage is a vital although virtually forgotten word. She has the courage to take a clear, strong stand on and for her beliefs.

And Ann Landers has fortitude, which is the counterpart of courage. She is willing to accept and is ready to bear the consequences of her courage and the consequences of her beliefs.

Her courage has supported and comforted thousands of people who are baffled and dismayed by the problems they face.

Eppie's demands on her associates are great, but her demands on herself are outrageous. Each day she pours quantities of compassionate energy into her letters and her column. From the first column she ever wrote to the one in her typewriter as you are reading this paragraph, Eppie has insisted that each letter which calls for an answer deserves, and therefore receives, the best answer she can devise.

In addition to her courage, fortitude, ability and insight, there are at least two unique distinctions Eppie brings to her work, to her column and to her book.

First, she never hesitates to call upon any individual anywhere who might help her provide a better answer to the questions she is asked.

Second, and of greatest importance, each answer is specifically designed to help the individual who asks the question. If the answer helps another or amuses another, it does so as a by-product. Her sole objective is to help the person who asks the question.

"Since You Ask Me" is not only by Ann Landers, it is Ann Landers herself, in fact, and in every sense. And as Ann Landers, it is Esther Pauline Lederer. And as Esther Pauline Lederer, it is Eppie. For Eppie wrote every word of it and Eppie believes every word of it. It is a good book because each of us will see himself reflected in some part of it; because some of us will see ourselves reflected in a considerable part of it; and, further, because all of us will see examples of others who have done more or who have endured more than we can conceive possible.

That the Ann Landers column has been a phenomenal newspaper success is beyond doubt. But the true measure of Eppie is that she has grown along with her column. In helping countless readers, she has developed her own knowledge and understanding of the behavior and motivations of all of us, whoever we are and wherever we may be.

For these and for a multitude of other reasons, Eppie has the deep affection and great respect of each of her associates.

Wilbur C. Munnecke
Vice President and General Manager, the
Chicago Sun-Times and the *Chicago Daily News*

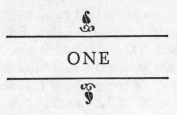

ONE

May I tell you about my operation?

> "Man that is born of woman is of few days—
> and full of trouble."　　　　　*Job 14:1*

THIS BOOK is about trouble—that uninvited guest who visits us all. Trouble is the common denominator of living. It is the great equalizer.

Trouble is no respecter of age, financial standing, social position or academic status. Trouble comes to people in high and low places alike. It is not a sign of stupidity, weakness, or bad luck. It is evidence that we are card-carrying members of the human race. As someone once put it, "only the living have problems."

This book is also about how to prevent trouble and what to do about it when you can't prevent it.

Since I've been writing the Ann Landers column, I've

learned a great deal about people and trouble. Among other things, I now know that millions of Americans earn an academy award every day of their lives for their acting ability. I've received thousands of letters from people who struggle heroically to present a cheerful face to the world. They give no hint of the civil war that rages within. How telling are the words of Lin Yutang, "Americans must be a very unhappy people. They laugh so much."

In the past six years more than half a million people have written to me about their troubles. The people who write range from six years of age to ninety-six. They live on suburban estates and they live in city slums. Some of my correspondents are members of the double-domed, egghead set and others are poorly educated, semi-literates whose labored efforts to express themselves are touchingly impressive. Many letters are funny; many are written in ink diluted with tears.

I've received letters from bank presidents, truck drivers, doctors, waitresses, coal miners, school teachers, factory workers, lawyers, artists, nuclear scientists, prostitutes, teen-agers and clergymen.

Their questions involve every phase of daily living. I've been asked by a disillusioned groom what to do about a young bride who boiled the envelope of grated cheese, instead of the macaroni.

A bewildered mother asked how to deal with her enterprising ten-year-old son who took a fistful of his father's two-dollar neckties to school and sold them for a dime apiece.

A mother of five young children asked:

"What can I do with a husband who consults his horoscope every morning? If the prediction for the day isn't good, he stays home from work."

A twenty-one-year-old girl who signed herself "Still Pure Bride" wanted to know what to do about her twenty-four-year-old husband who was sunburned on the first day of their honeymoon. Although the sunburn had been healed for weeks, he continued to smear medicine on his back as an excuse to keep his distance from her.

One reader simply asked:

> "*Dear Ann Landers:* Please tell me what is life? Thank you."

I've been asked how to handle mooching relatives, lecherous bosses, free-loading fiancés, noisy neighbors, jealous husbands, catty girl friends and pathological liars.

A woman from Little Rock sent a dozen snapshots of her gentleman friend and wanted to know if I thought he was dyeing his hair.

People have asked me if they should change churches, have another baby, run for public office, submit to nose surgery, marry for money, tell a close friend her husband is cheating, and hit a neighbor's child "when he's got it coming."

Every letter I receive gets a personal reply in the mail if there's a return address and I have eight full-time assistants helping me to tote that bale. I consider this personal service an obligation, not only to the troubled ones who write for advice, but to the newspapers that print my column.

Giving advice is an imposing responsibility and I am aware of the faith and trust placed in me by millions of readers. Had I been blessed with the wisdom of Solomon, I could not pull out of my hat the answers to all the questions put to me in a single day. I don't pretend to be an authority on every subject, but through the years I have been privileged to count authorities in many professions among my friends. When I want help with special problems involving such fields as medicine, psychiatry, law, religion, business, politics or education, I can turn to my friends who are experts and get first-rate advice. They may be thousands of miles away, but they are as close to me as my telephone.

People sometimes accuse me of making up letters because "those things just don't happen." Occasionally I print such an accusation:

> "*Dear Ann Landers:* I've been reading your column for a long time and I enjoy it a lot, but I'm sure you must make up the letters. Nobody could be so stupid as to get into the jams I read about in your column. I'm not complaining, mind you, it's good entertainment. Your column alone is worth the price of the newspaper, but I had to let you know I'm reading you regularly with tongue in cheek.
>
> X-Ray Ed"

> "*Dear X-Ray:* Thanks for the vote of no confidence. It bothers me not at all that you think I invent the letters. You aren't the only one.
>
> "What did you think, Ed, about the woman who sued her husband for divorce because he insisted that she pay him (out of her household budget) union-scale wages for emptying the garbage and doing odd jobs around the house? If you recall, he was an $18,000 a year vice-president of a bank.
>
> "And how about the man who divorced his wife because she insisted he wear a chauffeur's uniform and wait outside when she went visiting and shopping?
>
> "And what about the New York woman who had a money fight with her husband, went to the bank, drew out $7,100 in 50 and 100 dollar bills from their joint bank

account and threw the money around on a Manhattan street corner—to the delight of passers-by.

"Good entertainment? Well, these incidents aren't from my column, Buster. They're recent news stories.

"Human nature being what it is, it would be a waste of time to fabricate letters. Manufactured situations would be pale, indeed compared with what people are *really* up to.

Ann Landers"

Of course, I get some phony letters, but the percentage of oddball and pornographic mail is surprisingly small (less than 4 per cent of the total).

I've become adept at spotting phony letters, and although I'm fooled occasionally, it doesn't happen often. The phony letters are usually neatly prepared manuscripts and the story unfolds like a novel. The author is often a frustrated amateur who longs to see his literary brainchild in print.

Troubled people don't write masterpieces. The real story is rarely told in proper chronological order. Often, important details are written in the margin, having been forgotten in the first telling.

The worried and upset writer misspells simple words, frequently runs out of ink and finishes in pencil. Many letters conclude:

"I'm sorry this is such a messy looking thing, Ann, but I'm afraid if I take the time to write it over I'll lose my nerve and never mail it. It took an awful lot out of me to write it the way it is. Please help me right away."

And I do try to help them right away (if the problem seems especially urgent I send a telegram). I receive handmade gifts from people who can't afford to buy a present but they want me to know they appreciate the advice. When I lectured recently in Columbus, Ohio, a reader surprised me with a lovely oil portrait of "his favorite columnist." It was waiting for me in my hotel suite, elegantly displayed on an easel.

Several months ago I received a china cup and saucer, a jar of instant coffee, a bag of sugar, a tin of condensed cream and a spoon. The package came from a Toronto reader who explained in an accompanying letter that he wanted to buy me a cup of coffee because I had given him such useful advice on a problem which involved his teenage daughter.

Although no two problems are identical because no two people are identical, human problems fall into definite patterns. Obviously, problems are often related, one being the outgrowth of another.

The problem of alcoholism, for example, invariably hatches a multitude of other problems. The man who drinks excessively usually has financial troubles because he spends the rent and grocery money in the taverns. He is frequently out of work because he takes too much time off to dry out. The alcoholic is apt to have marital trouble for obvious reasons.

A common thread is woven into every messed up life. It is fear. What are we afraid of? We're afraid of the boss. We're afraid our husbands (or wives) are cheating. If we are cheating, we're afraid of getting caught. We're afraid of business failure, social snubs, in-laws, what the neighbors will think. We're afraid of getting old; we are afraid of getting sick.

I was originally drawn to the advice field because it seemed like a good way to help people, but I had no idea how many frightened, stumbling, driven people need help. I was saddened to discover that thousands of people view life as "the enemy." They dread the dawn of a new day. I was shocked at the number of weary souls who drag their ulcers and migraines to work every morning. I had no idea so many American women are kitchen drinkers who attempt to escape reality by drinking themselves into semiconsciousness.

The breakdown of my mail is an enlightening barometer of the day-to-day pressures imposed upon us by our society. Almost half the letters come from men. Teen-agers, mostly girls, contribute heavily. The remaining mail is largely from women who are having trouble with their marriages. Surprisingly few people write to me about money problems.

Many people who write for advice don't really want it. They simply want to unload. Putting the ᶜtory down on paper is excellent therapy for a heavy heart. A businessman who signed himself "Smart Too Late" wrote:

> *"Dear Ann Landers:* I know you can't untangle the mess I've made of my life, but if I don't talk to someone I'll blow my top."

The man went on to tell of an illicit love affair with his wife's best friend. He was tortured by guilt, and the guilt became unbearable when he was informed that he had been named Father of the Year and was to receive an award at a civic banquet.

I advised the father to accept the award and then live up to it. Guilt is erosive and more than anything, this man needed to stop beating himself and to find a positive, constructive approach to his marriage.

Occasionally a reader will criticize me for injecting humor into my column. "People's troubles are no laughing matter" I've been told in an admonishing tone. No one knows this better than I, but I know, too, that humor sometimes takes the sting out of misery. The humor in my column is never intentionally cruel; I never insult or make fun of the person with the problem. And I never sacrifice sound advice for a laugh.

My newspaper column affords me the opportunity to offer, in capsule form, advice on almost every phase of living. Newspaper writers are forever fighting the space problem, and the most challenging aspect of my work is to pack into a few lines sensible and useful advice expressed in understandable, lunch-bucket language.

I love writing a daily advice column, and I had no aspirations to branch out and write a book about people's problems. My readers, however, changed my mind. They told me they clipped columns from their newspapers and pasted them into scrap books so if the problem arose again they could refer to the advice. They suggested it would be enormously useful if they could turn to an Ann Landers book for guidance in dealing with life's problems. So I decided to write this book.

I am not attempting to substitute for the psychiatrist, the analyst, the doctor, the clergyman, the marriage counselor, the social worker or the lawyer. In fact, I urge thousands of people every month to seek professional help for counsel and therapy. We have a complete file on service agencies in every city in which my column is printed. We often suggest that readers go to the nearest city if the town they live in does not have counseling facilities. We supply them with the address and telephone number and in some cases, the name of the person to see.

We have received many warm and gratifying letters from case workers and directors of agencies who keep us informed of the progress of people we have sent to them. The most rewarding letters come from alcoholics who have found their way to sobriety through Alcoholics Anonymous. A reader from Dallas wrote:

"I was a gutter bum, a worthless drunk. I read a letter in your column about a guy who went A.A. His problems sounded so much like mine I decided to give A.A. a try. You'll be happy to know I have been sober for three months and I'm sure I have it licked."

The most pathetic letters come from unmarried pregnant girls who are frantic and fearful and don't know what to do, or where to go. We have a complete list of homes for unwed mothers and we direct the girls without delay. One girl wrote:

"Thank you for sending me to the Florence Crittenton Home. I never knew there were people like this in the whole world. If it hadn't been for you I would have walked into the lake."

So now, after six years and more than half a million letters, this human wailing wall has put the sum of her experience between hard covers. It is my earnest hope that this book will help you to recognize your troubles—whatever they may be—as an inevitable, inescapable part of life. I hope it will shed a little light in some darkened corner, plant hope where there is despair, replace fear with courage and perhaps open a few doors to self-understanding.

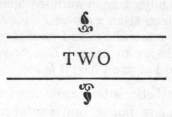

TWO

Whistles and thistles

IN EVERY BATCH of mail there are surprises, explosive reactions to innocent statements, cries of foul, and tenderly worded bouquets. A letter printed in the column which evokes a warm "God bless you" from a reader in Hillsdale, Michigan, may move a Fort Lauderdale husband to write "your advice is lousy. Drop dead."

My daily readers are unpredictable, super-sensitive, warm hearted, critical, and fiercely loyal. They are the writin'est, hatin'est, lovin'est cross-section of humanity in all the world—and happiest when they catch me in an error. They praise me lavishly when they agree and they slice me to ribbons if I trample on a pet theory.

As I cut through the Everest of mail facing me every day, I keep a third eye open for potential column material. I try to select letters which cut across the interests of a wide variety of readers. I never select a letter because I think it will pull mail. It is impossible to predict which letter will produce what response. Why certain letters and not others trigger volumes of mail is a mystery. I am no closer to understanding it today than I was six years ago when I wrote my first column.

I experienced my first brush with the strongest union in the world—"The American Sisterhood of Housewives"—within weeks after I had become Ann Landers. A man from Marshalltown, Iowa wrote:

> "I am a mail carrier. My job starts at 8:30 in the morning. In my opinion this is time enough for the American woman to slip on a dress and run a comb through her hair. You'd be shocked if you knew how many women answer the door in their nightgowns and barefooted. Please say something to let these slobs know they have an obligation to the people who have to look at them."

I thought I disposed of him (however ungrammatically) with this: "You ain't never been a woman at 8:30 in the morning."

But the homemakers of America had no intention of letting the scoundrel off with a light tap on the wrist! Hundreds of letters from all over the country poured in. The women wrote detailed accounts of what needs to be done every morning to get a husband off to work and kids off to school.

"Slip on a dress, indeed," bellowed an irate Detroit mother. "It's more important that I put on the baby's formula, get the coffee going, fix the oatmeal, pack the lunch buckets, check the kids for handkerchiefs, books, bus fare and see that their shoes are on the right feet."

A woman in Toledo ended the rhubarb with:

> "My husband is a mailman. I'll bet anything he wrote you that letter. He's a fine one to talk about slobs. You ought to see *him* on his day off."

The enthusiasm with which readers jump to the rescue of someone who asks for help always surprises me. A simple plea from a woman who was having trouble making gelatin molds created a small-scale crisis in the Chicago post office.

The defeated housewife wrote:

> "All my friends seem to have such amazing luck with their gelatin molds. Some of them can even make it in three colors! My gelatin mold is either too rubbery or too loose. The fruit either floats on top or it sinks to the bottom. It's giving me an inferiority complex."

Having experienced similar failures with gelatin molds I sympathized with her and invited readers to send in suggestions for us both. Within the week we received over a thousand letters containing helpful hints on how to make a perfect gelatin mold.

I once spent two days with obstetricians and lawyers to learn how long it takes to produce a baby. I always had been under the impression that it takes nine months, but my readers planted serious doubts in my mind.

It all started when a young man wrote that he had married "in a hurry" when his girl friend told him she was pregnant.

> "Eighteen months have passed," he wrote. "My wife has gained 40 pounds, she's been wearing maternity clothes for over a year, but there's no sign of a baby. She insists this is just a long pregnancy. Is it *possible* for a woman to be pregnant for eighteen months?"

I had to tell the young man that it sounded like a case of excellent salesmanship with no product to back up the pitch.

My reply opened the floodgates. I was bombarded with

letters from hundreds of women who insisted their pregnancies ran from 10 to 22 months. (The majority of these women had "long-term" babies after their husbands had left for overseas.) The winner and still champion was a woman in Kentucky who claimed she had been pregnant for four years. I wrapped up the free-for-all by printing this:

> "In most humans the average pregnancy is from 270 to 290 days. In cases where there is no supporting medical history but where legal status is important the courts have made the following decision: French law holds that the husband is the father if a child is born as late as 300 days after the death of the husband. German laws allows 320 days. British law grants 331 days. American law is modeled after the British, so 331 days is the limit in this country. Women who claim longer pregnancies aren't necessarily trying to put one over. The count can be thrown off for a variety of reasons. But it's like I said, ladies—most pregnancies are nine months. It just *seems* longer."

A Des Moines mother wrote that she was having an affair with the plumber who lived next door. "I got involved," she admitted, "when I tried to get faucet handles at a reduced rate." She added this practical thought:

> "It's wonderful having him so near. Whenever anything goes wrong with the plumbing, he comes right over and fixes it for nothing. I save a lot of money this way but if my husband knew he'd brain me."

I advised her to break off with the man at once, or she could wind up with the most expensive faucet handles on record. I also suggested that when anything goes wrong with her pipes she should hire a plumber and pay him union wages. Dozens of plumbers wrote to say thanks. (A few plumbers' wives expressed their appreciation, too.)

The Chicago Journeymen Plumbers' Union, Local 130, made me an honorary member.

One unforgettable experience was the "battle of the bedsheets." A wife who signed herself "Four Poster" wrote that she had put brand new sheets on the bed and that this had led to real trouble. Her husband raved about the luxurious texture of the sheets but he added a dangerous phrase, "Why aren't they like this all the time—Mother's were." The wife informed him that his mother probably ironed her sheets but *she* had no intention of doing so. A hot argument followed during which he called her a few choice names. She wrote to ask if I thought a wife ought to iron bedsheets.

I replied "Yes, if ironed sheets mean so much to your husband, it's worth 30 minutes a week to make him happy." I added a homey touch by suggesting that she be thankful her marital troubles could be ironed out so easily.

For this advice I was labeled a traitor to my sex and a double-crossing rat. A woman in Utica, New York, closed her scathing letter with this:

> "It's easy for you to sit there in your fancy apartment in Chicago, Ann Landers, and think of ways for ordinary housewives to kill themselves with more work. I'll bet you never ironed a bedsheet in your life."

I told the Utica reader that I had ironed a good many bedsheets in my life. "In fact," I proclaimed in print, "if all the bedsheets I have ironed were placed end to end they'd probably reach from Chicago to Utica."

My reply quieted the women, but it woke up the men. It seemed that almost every male who had completed high school math sat down and figured out the number of miles between Utica and Chicago. They then figured the length of the average bedsheet and the time it would take to iron it. The mathematics clobbered me. A professor at the University of Pittsburgh let me know I would have had to iron 55 bedsheets every day for the past 60 years. In the face of such statistics I confessed I had taken a wild guess. I named my own punishment—ten lashes with a wet bedsheet.

Teen-agers let me have it with both barrels whenever I "betray" them. For instance: I took the position that twelve- and thirteen-year-olds are too young for boy-girl dances. I was tagged as "hopelessly square," "a kook," and "very old-fashioned."

Teen-agers are a forgiving lot, however. The very next day I'm a "good egg," a "living doll," and "real great"—especially when I advise mothers to stay out of their daughters' diaries and keep their cotton pickin' hands off the kids' mail.

I almost reopened the Civil War when I told an obviously jealous Northern woman that there's nothing uneducated about a Southern accent, that, in fact, I find it feminine and charming. For some mysterious reason many women from New York and New Jersey (particularly White Plains and Newark) were irritated by my reply and allowed as how I was either from the South myself or my husband had some "interests" down there.

Occasionally I've reversed my advice after readers have persuaded me I was wrong. The case of the crocheted dress is one I'll never forget. A distraught Seattle mother wrote that Granny had spent six months crocheting a dress for her ten-year-old grandchild to wear to a family reunion. The mother wrote that the dress was unattractive and old-fashioned . . . "Ann, you know kids don't wear crocheted dresses any more." On the other hand, Granny was eighty-two years old, well-meaning and sensitive. She would be crushed if the little girl didn't wear her crocheted dress to the family reunion. What should be done? This was a tough one, but I advised the mother to explain to the child that the dress was a labor of love—that Granny's feelings were more important than looking up-to-the-minute this one night of the year. I told her to explain that everyone would know she was wearing the dress to be kind and it was more important to be kind than to be stylish.

Well, I thought this was pretty good advice, but my readers did not. A blizzard of letters blew in from all over the country. The readers were against me 100 to 1.

A designer from California wired "For Lord's sake, Ann Landers, have a heart. Don't make the kid wear that ugly crocheted dress!" I received patterns. People sent me drawings. A mother from Fairbanks, Alaska, wrote:

> "Send the dress to me. I will make a pink taffeta lining and overskirt and it will be lovely."

A reader from Buffalo sent three dollars with a request that I buy some red satin ribbon for the crocheted dress and send it to the mother. The most amusing letter came from an eleven-year-old boy who lives in Phoenix. He wrote:

> "I feel very sorry for that little girl, and I think I can help her. My father owns a dry cleaning shop. If she will send the dress to *him*, he will ruin it for her."

The letter that produced the greatest number of anguished screams was from a Chicago father. He said he was sick of taking his three sons downtown for haircuts and chewing up a ten-dollar bill. "Chicago Pop," as he signed himself, suggested parents of large families demand that the price of haircuts be reduced, or alternatively, that they boycott barbers and buy do-it-yourself kits and cut the kids' hair at home.

I received over two thousand letters from barbers, their wives, sweethearts, and children. I had to devote not one but two columns to the blistering rebuttals. Here are some samples from the mail:

From Chicago: "If I had 'Chicago Pop' in my chair for five minutes I'd give him a haircut he'd never recover from. If a barber clears $100 a week he's lucky. Barbers get no vacation, no pension, no bonus, and no group insurance. If haircuts had kept pace with the cost of living, they'd be five dollars, not two dollars."

From Salem, Oregon: "Have you ever heard of a wealthy barber?" I replied "Yes. Perry Como" (and promptly received a raft of letters complaining about that wisecrack).

From Troy: "A friend gave me one of those home kits and I followed the 'simple instructions.' The kids' heads looked like three miles of bad road. They refused to go to school and we had to buy stocking caps for them. My advice is pay the barber the two dollars!"

From Seattle: "My dad is a barber. His right elbow is stiffening from holding it in the air so much. His legs are in terrible condition from standing so long. He needs an operation but can't take the time away from the chair."

From Akron: "The hardest part of barbering is listening to nutty chatter all day. You ought to hear the things people tell barbers. There are sure a lot of loons in this world."

By the time I finished with the barber mail, I was persuaded that the haircut was the best buy in all of America and that the price should be increased.

Second only to the barbers in their ability to articulate are homeowners who entertain in their basements. The explosion was set off by a Philadelphia reader who signed herself "Seven Leagues Under."

"What has happened to American entertaining?" she wrote. "I refer to people who invite you over for a social evening and put you in the cellar—pardon me, the recreation room. It's insulting, and I for one am tired of sitting on beat-up couches and looking at oil burners, clothes lines and ratty rugs."

I told "Seven Leagues" she had a point. Some recreation rooms are lovely but the upstairs is usually nicer and, in my opinion, that's where guests should be entertained.

Hundreds of homeowners took this as a personal insult and let me know that *their* basements were nicer than most people's living rooms. A few readers wrote in praise of underground entertainment for a reason which had never occurred to me. I had to admit they, too, had a point. Said one . . .

> "I'm one of those 'lowbrows' who entertains in the basement and I'm darned thankful for such a place. My husband plays poker with a bunch of baboons who don't have sense enough to use an ashtray. The old table they use has three dozen cigarette burns. My sisters have a total of fourteen kids who walk on coffee tables and get gum and candy on furniture. Even the junk down there is too good for them. If Eleanor Roosevelt or the president of Harvard came over I might invite them into my living room, but for the crumby crowd we go around with the cellar is good enough."

One of the most fascinating encounters with my readers might be called "the case of the electronic bridgework." I received a letter from a woman who told me she was worried about her mother-in-law. It seems the older woman insisted she was receiving radio messages through her bridgework.

"Of late," the daughter-in-law wrote, "Mother swears she is intercepting, through her teeth, secret messages between Russia and Red China. She wants to go to the F.B.I."

Although I always research problems about which there may be a question, this one sounded like a sure case of overactive imagination. I felt safe in suggesting psychiatric care. Soon after the letter and my advice appeared in print I received telephone calls and letters informing me that I had done the woman a terrible injustice because it certainly was possible to "tune in through the teeth."

Before the week was out I had stacks of letters from readers recounting their own experiences with bridgework reception and it seemed that almost everyone in the country was wired for sound but me.

An irate reader from Watertown, South Dakota, wrote:

> "It is entirely possible that the woman is bringing in messages on her bridgework. For years I was afraid to tell anybody I was getting messages through my teeth. I finally told my dentist and he said when a person has a certain type of metal filling, a sensitive jaw bone could act as a conductor and carry the vibrations to the brain."

A man in New Jersey wrote "I've been getting Station WOR in New York regularly." Readers informed me that they also received dance music and commercials through their hearing aids, dental braces, bobby pins and steam radiators. After a while I began to feel underprivileged. I have had hundreds of dollars worth of dental work and I wasn't getting any entertainment whatever.

Dr. Morris Brodwin, Associate Professor of Electrical Engineering at Northwestern University, set the record straight for me.

"It is possible," he said, "that fillings in the mouth may act as a radio receiving set exciting the nerves which, in turn, may be interpreted by the brain as 'noise' or intelligence. However, these reports have not been thoroughly investigated by competent scientists and consequently no firm explanation of the physical basis for this phenomenon can be given."

I was armed for the next letter from a Hartford, Connecticut, clubwoman, which read:

"About that woman who was intercepting messages through her bridgework—I'd like to tell you what happened to me along the same lines. I kept hearing voices, too, but I was afraid to say anything. You know how people are about things like that. Finally I couldn't stand it so I told my doctor. He asked me if I could identify the voices and I told him that I was sure Sir Francis Drake was communicating with me. He recommended a psychiatrist. I went to the psychiatrist for three years and the voice stopped. Now, since I read that letter in your column, I am sure I was communicating with Sir Francis Drake and I certainly would like to re-establish the connection. I miss him."

Despite these out-of-the-ordinary examples, my daily mail reflects life as millions of people live it. And an authentic reflection it is, too. Every batch of mail demonstrates that the human animal can be noble, magnanimous, ruthless, punishing and sometimes brainless. I never know which envelope will contain a glittering example of man at his best, or a depressing picture of man at his worst. But no day at my desk is without a heart-tug or a nugget of solid gold laughter.

One of the great satisfactions of this work is to know that every day—365 days a year—I can bring millions of people together, to share a common experience—or an uncommon one. I do not feel that my counsel is invalidated because it is sometimes offered with a light touch. Advice spliced with humor is not only more palatable, but it is more effective. Perhaps it is true as Nietzsche said, "Man suffers so excruciatingly that he was compelled to invent laughter."

THREE

How to pick a winner

SINCE MARRIAGE is probably the most important single decision of a lifetime, it is strange that so many people rush into it with less selectivity than they would give to the choice of a secondhand car, or a winter coat.

My desk is stacked with letters that start something like this:

> "Dear Ann Landers: I'm ready to call it quits. We've been married two years and all we do is fight. I was so crazy about Bill when we were going together nobody could tell me anything. My folks tried, but I told them to mind their own business and let me run my life. When Bill and I were dating, our sex life was wonderful. Now I hate for him to come near me. What happened to the great love affair of the century?"

An equally distressing letter from a disillusioned twenty-two-year-old husband started like this:

> "I've been married three years to a girl who is now twenty. She quit high school to marry me. It was her own

idea, but she blames me for ruining her chance to get an education. She didn't know one thing about being a wife when we got married, but I thought she'd learn. Well, she hasn't even tried. The house looks like a pigpen. She fixes sandwiches for dinner, or opens tin cans. All she wants to do is go roller skating with her girl friends. On my wedding day, I was the happiest guy in the world. What went wrong?"

I had to tell the poor fellow, as I have told hundreds of the disenchanted, that *all* marriages are happy, it's living together afterward that's tough.

Thousands of letters from unhappily married people suggest one striking reason for failure. Young romanticists spin themselves into a cocoon of dreams and imagine that life together is going to be like the marriages they've seen in the movies, on TV screens, and in the ads for engagement rings and silverware.

Unfortunately, a great many American movies are a far cry from life as people live it. How many husbands in the movies get up in the morning and go to work? I recall precious few. The blissfully happy couple live in a beautifully furnished home. They wear lovely clothes, drive expensive cars and are forever going to formal parties, but nobody goes to work. If there are children, they are never underfoot, sick, or in soiled play clothes. The maid or governess ushers them into the drawing room for a good-night kiss and shepherds them out again. The movie wife is seldom seen wrestling with bills, shopping for groceries, harassed by troublesome relatives or involved in anything so mundane as housework. The central problem in most movie marriages is the other woman who is (naturally) younger and more beautiful than the wife. The other woman is sometimes married to an attractive man, who doesn't work either.

The ads for engagement rings say "forever," but the statistics show that the divorce rate in America is at an all-time high. The chances for a lasting marriage today are approximately one half what they were 30 years ago.

The silverware ads picture an attractive male in an Ivy League suit. His dewy-eyed bride greets him at the garden gate. She is dainty in her crisp little house dress, and she has a daisy in her hair. Is it any wonder our young people expect marriage to be a beautiful song that never ends, an adventure in fairyland? Everywhere they look (except at home) marriage is heavenly.

When I speak to high school audiences, I emphasize the realities of married life. I tell the teen-agers that marriage is the difficult business of living with another human being. It's in-laws, doctor bills, car payments, dishes in the sink, and mortgages. It's disappointment and diaper rash. It's the raise or promotion that he almost, but never quite gets. It's tears in the pillow at night.

If teen-agers were given facts instead of fiction, they might be less eager to trade their bobby socks for satin wedding slippers. And they would be less shaken and bewildered when faced with some of the not-so-attractive aspects of married life. The young bride who discovers that her "dream boat" actually snores feels as if she's been robbed. One bride married less than three weeks wrote:

> "I can't discuss this with anyone I know personally because I'm too ashamed. How come in the morning my husband has a beard?"

Love is great but let's be practical

Remember that no marriage is free of problems. Be realistic, not only about marriage itself, but about the person you are considering as a lifetime partner. Remember that dating couples usually see each other in the most flattering light. An aura of saintliness surrounds the beloved. While love may not be blind, its vision is something other than 20–20. In the mind's eye of a high school girl, the football hero may be the most exciting prize in all the world. But the football season doesn't last forever and unless her halfback can back up his handsome physique with manly character qualities, he's a poor marriage risk. The glamour of high school and college athletics has lured many foolish girls into ill-fated marriages.

One such wife from Minneapolis wrote:

> "I married the campus hero. I felt lucky to get him. The girls in the sorority house envied me. He was so good looking and big. I felt like a feather in his arms. My father told me he was a lunkhead and that he wouldn't treat me right. When he stood me up on dates, my dad boiled. I protected him by manufacturing excuses. Now after eight years of marriage, I'm fed up with his selfish ways. He puts himself before me and the kids in everything. His greatest pleasure in life is to show off his scrapbook and talk about his college days."

My plea for realism among young couples who fancy themselves in love has met with lively opposition, particularly among university students. Many coeds with whom I spoke at Southern Methodist University in Dallas, criticized my concern as "materialistic and calculating."

"Projection is of prime importance," I told them. "Try to imagine, temporarily, how you'll feel about that 'living doll' in 15 years, after his hair has fallen out and he has gained 30 pounds. Will you still be crazy about him even though his looks are gone and you have to use a secondhand washing machine and make do with last year's Easter hat?"

All people don't want the same things out of life, and

this is good. Some women are content with a man of limited horizons who wants to work 37½ hours a week for a modest salary. Others want an aggressive type, one who strives to scale financial, artistic or intellectual heights.

I make no plea for either the go-getter or the unambitious. I do plead, however, that those who are considering marriage think and plan ahead. You can accomplish this only by discussing goals and objectives during courtship. Decide what you want out of life and then choose someone who shares your dreams and objectives.

Many an unfortunate marriage could have been avoided if the two parties had discussed frankly, in advance, what each one wanted. Here is an example:

> "My husband won't be satisfied until he has all the money in the world. He works 16 hours a day. He's a stranger to his children. I may as well be a widow for all the help he gives me. This beautiful home we live in doesn't mean a thing. I'd rather live in three rooms and have my husband with me evenings."

The other side of the coin looks like this:

> "Joe has no ambition. He could add 40 per cent to his income if he'd work Saturdays and a few evenings a week. But no, he'd rather take the kids fishing or fool around in the garage with his junky sports car. I tell him there's more to being a father than playing baseball with the kids in the backyard. If he had any gumption, he'd earn a little overtime so the girls could have decent clothes and the boys could have new bikes instead of secondhand ones. Our kids will never go to college unless they put themselves through. We haven't got two cents to our name."

The lesson in these contrasting letters is this: Decide what is important, then choose someone who shares those concepts. A solid marriage is based on reality. Dream castles are lovely to visit, but don't make the mistake of trying to live in them permanently. It won't work.

What's your hurry?

A great many divorces could have been prevented had the couple gone together another 90 days. They would have become better acquainted, and probably would not have embarked on marriage in the first place.

In much of the mail these words appear: "I'm mad about him. It was love at first sight." I advise them to look again, they may see things they hadn't noticed before. Love at first sight is a myth, in spite of the poets' claims. Love does not konk you on the head like a chunk of loose plaster. It must take root and grow, a day at a time. Happily married people who claim they fell in love at first sight didn't really. They were smitten on first meeting and the fine qualities they imagined they saw proved to be present after they got to know each other.

Frequently a purely chemical reaction is mistaken for love. One college freshman wrote:

"I know it's love. Whenever I see her, my knees turn to water and my heart pounds like a triphammer. It's got to be love. It can't be anything else."

A strong physical reaction is a powerful plus and should be a factor in the final selection. But a compelling sexual attraction is not a substantial hook on which to hang a marriage. And this is where so many "madly in love" couples who marry in a hurry make their greatest mistake. They are unable to distinguish between love and sex. They learn too late that they can't live their entire lives in the bedroom. A lusty young groom may be less critical of a scorched collar if his love life is exciting, but after the first fires of romance have receded the husband views his marriage with less heat and more light. When the "great lover" begins to notice that buttons are missing from his shirt and that his wife doesn't cook (she merely defrosts), the accumulation of irritations would make even the current sex symbol less attractive.

This letter from Albany, New York, illustrates the tragedy of a too hasty (and too early) marriage:

"I'm nineteen and my divorce will be final next week. I'm writing to find out where I failed. I'm still young and hope to marry again, but I don't want to make the same mistake. Stu and I started to go together in our senior year of high school. He was my first serious sweetheart. We tried to keep our feelings under control, but it was no use. After three months of going steady and being together all the time, we couldn't control ourselves. It was pure heaven when we were together, even though we had to sneak around a lot.

"We got married two months after high school graduation. I went to work in a candy shop and he got a job in a garage. For about four months we were blissfully happy. Then I noticed that the sex interest was slacking off, for both of us. He'd tell me he was worn out from a hard day at the garage, and I'd fib about having a headache. After six months of pretending we had a frank talk. He told me I was a nice person but he didn't love me and the thrill had gone out of our marriage. I confessed I felt the same way about him. We parted friends and I filed for divorce. Please tell me what was wrong. We were so in love."

I told the nineteen-year-old divorcée that I saw no evidence of love in their relationship. Their marriage was based on physical desire, a frail plank on which to build a life together. When their sexual appetites reached the saturation point, their great "love" had had it. The forbidden aspect of the romance made it glamourous and exciting, but when their love-making became legal they lost interest.

Pre-marital experimentation can stunt the growth of a relationship. When a couple shares intimacies too early in the game, they usually stop talking, and stop learning about each other. Physical contact becomes more thrilling than conversation, and the lines of emotional and spiritual communication begin to break down.

There is no substitute for time in testing the durability of a relationship. A couple should go together long enough to view each other in a variety of circumstances. Complaints of this nature are numerous:

> "I never knew until after we were married that he had such a violent temper" . . . "I was shocked to find he was such a mama's boy" . . . "I wasn't aware that he couldn't stand children."

Men complain similarly:

> "I didn't know she was such a liar" . . . "I had no idea she drank in the daytime too" . . . "I didn't know she was so lazy."

Although it is impossible to know all about a person until you share a life together under a single roof a great many things can be learned during courtship if a couple will take the time. It's easy to be charming when life goes well, but how does he behave when the going is rocky? Is he dependable? Does he have patience? Is he considerate? Is he understanding? Is he honest? The individual who conducts himself with maturity under stress will make a reliable marriage partner. So time—time to test him in the clutch—can be your greatest ally.

What can you share?

The more you have in common with the person you marry the better your chances for a successful marriage. Although there are notable exceptions (we all have our pet examples), couples who share similar economic, religious, racial, and educational backgrounds have fewer marital problems. The reason is obvious. There are fewer areas of conflict, fewer things to fight about.

There's an old joke that if the rich girls married poor boys and the rich boys married poor girls, the money would be spread around and poverty would be abolished. This is a delightful theory, but the experts know that marriages of people from opposite ends of the economic spectrum often fail.

Few principles are more deeply embedded in our society than the right to marry whom we please, and the suggestion that economic status should be considered may sound downright un-American. But problems are bound to crop up when two people who have been reared differently undertake to share a life. Surprisingly enough, my mail indicates that the partner with the money is seldom the trouble maker. The one who marries wealth usually creates the problems. He is unable to shake off a feeling of inferiority and often attempts to get off the defensive by attacking. The following lines written by a San Francisco woman illustrate the point:

> "Ted's family had nothing. My family was prominent in social and financial circles. He said we were from different worlds, but I assured him our love could bridge the gap. I was willing to live on his salary which meant doing without many things I'd been accustomed to. The trouble began on our honeymoon. He accused my parents of putting on a ridiculously lavish wedding to flaunt their wealth.

He said his family felt out of place and it was my family's fault. After a few months his needling became intolerable. He'd look at me and say 'You miss going to the club, don't you?' I'd say 'No.' He'd call me a liar and I'd end up in tears. This sort of cruelty went on for two years. Finally I got so thin and nervous, I knew that if I didn't leave him I'd have a complete breakdown. When I packed and went home, everyone said 'She couldn't take it. He couldn't make enough money to keep her satisfied.' I'm not writing for advice—it's too late for that. I'm writing to let you know that a marriage between the haves and have-nots can be a terrible uphill fight, but not for the reasons most people imagine."

Educational background is an important factor often ignored when two people fancy themselves in love. One young man wrote:

"If I had been listening to the girl instead of just looking at her, I might have avoided this horrible mistake. She is a doll with a sawdust head."

Many of the letters from teen-agers who want to quit high school to go to work or get married sound as if they had all been written by the same person:

"School bores me; I'm not learning anything. I can get a job and earn good money and buy some nice clothes. Why should I stay in this dumb place?"

I urge them to stay in school and get that diploma no matter how boring and pointless it may seem. I tell them about the thousands who have written to say they could kick themselves for quitting—that it was the most foolish thing they ever did. I warn them of the nagging feeling of inferiority they'll inevitably experience.

Well-educated women who marry poorly educated men

seem not to notice the glaring grammatical defects and limited intellectual interests until after they've been married a few years. This always strikes me as odd. It's as if they had been totally deaf during courtship. One such situation was described by a Boston wife. She wrote:

> "The children ask me why Daddy says 'ex-scape' instead of 'escape' and 'have went.' When they ask him, he gets furious and accuses me of putting them up to it. In company his grammar is so bad it's embarrassing. Some of his sentences don't have verbs and no one can follow his conversation. He refuses to go to night school or hire a tutor. What can I do?"

I told her there was nothing she could do. The husband who resents being corrected and will make no effort to help himself is hopeless. Married people who write about such problems are advised to tolerate the ear-grating language in silence and concentrate instead on the positive qualities of the person. You can't divorce a man because he says "have went."

When engaged people write with this complaint, I warn them that if the beloved's poor grammar and lack of general knowledge is a thorn in the side during courtship, it is bound to be a bone in the throat after marriage.

Often in my column I use the phrase "marriage is not a reform school." The notion that a man or woman can be made over after marriage is pure poppycock. A young woman from Sheboygan, Wisconsin, who wrote "He drinks a little too much but promises to cut down after we are married" got this reply:

> "If he drinks 'a little too much' now, he'll probably drink a lot too much after you marry him. A man who won't keep the cork in the bottle for his sweetheart, certainly won't do it for his wife."

The young lady who orders the most expensive dinner on the menu, hints for costly gifts, and wants to go to high-priced places when she knows her boy friend is having a financial struggle is a poor marriage bet. She is not likely to be a frugal wife, willing to cut corners and do without. Instead, she will probably live up to the last dollar and keep him forever in debt.

When I receive letters from girls who confide "my fiancé lost his temper and slapped me a few times—shall I have a word with him?" I tell them by all means, and the word should be "Good-bye!" A woman who puts up with "a few slaps and punches" during courtship can expect loose bridgework and worse if she marries the man.

Superficial changes, however, are often made after marriage. A man may get his wife to cut her hair or let it grow, a woman may inveigle her husband into wearing more conservative neckties. But such minor triumphs have nothing to do with basic character. I urge engaged couples to take a good hard look at one another as they are now, because the husband or wife is going to be a great deal like the sweetheart, minus the halo and the wings.

In our society it is inevitable that people of different religious faiths fall in love and marry. It cannot be denied that some mixed marriages work out well, but the failures outnumber the successes. Rabbis, priests, and ministers have consistently opposed mixed marriages because they agree it's a difficult hurdle, and marriage has enough hurdles without adding this one.

Rabbi Stanley Rabinowitz of Washington, D.C., says in his pamphlet, *Love and Marriage*, that a study of 13,000 people in Maryland between the ages of 16 and 24 indicated:

Where both parents were Jewish, one out of 24 came from a broken home.

Where both parents were Catholic, it was one out of 16.

Where both parents were Protestant, it was one out of 15.

Where parents were of different religions, it was one out of 6.

The shakiest interfaith marriages involve a Protestant wife and a Catholic husband. The second most unsuccessful marriages are between Jewish husbands and Gentile wives. This combination occurs 20 times more often than the Jewish wife and the Gentile husband, which for some reason is a more lasting combination.

Psychiatrists tell us that the person who marries out of his faith may do so as an act of unconscious rebellion against his parents. The rebel may choose a partner who is "out of bounds" as a means of punishing a domineering mother or father. Some authorities claim that the ultimate in rebellion is conversion to another religion. It is a means of rejecting not only one's parents, but one's people and even one's God.

In my column I have taken an unqualified stand against interfaith dating and interfaith marriage. Sharp criticism has been the result, particularly from teen-agers who want to date outside their religion (frequently against the wishes of their parents). When they write to me for support, I tell them their parents are right and to listen to them. A teen-ager from Lafayette, Indiana, wrote:

> "My folks don't want me to go with Mike because he's Catholic. I say Catholics are just as good as anybody else. I think it's undemocratic to hold a person's religion against him. Please tell my folks they are narrow-minded and bigoted and that I should be allowed to pick my boy friends for character and brains and personality. Religion should be left out of it."

I advised the young woman that there's nothing undemocratic or bigoted about parents who want a solid and lasting marriage for their children. Teen-agers who date outside their religion clearly run the risk of marrying outside their religion. Mixed marriages have two strikes against them. Why look for trouble?

The mixed marriages that succeed are usually between two people who are lukewarm to religion and willing to settle for a third affiliation, or none at all. If one is devout and the other has no strong religious feelings, it is sometimes possible for the indifferent one to accept the faith of his beloved without feeling enslaved.

Often young people who claim to have no strong religious feelings and are willing to drift along with a mate of a different faith, change their minds after the children come along. One such situation was described in this letter from an Elmira, New York, man:

> "Religion was not discussed much in our family. I didn't think it was important. I married a Catholic girl who was so devout I used to tease her about being a fanatic. When we got married, I signed papers agreeing to raise our children in the Catholic faith. I never thought it would bother me, but I was mistaken. We have five kids now and all of them attend parochial school. It's costing me several hundred dollars a year which could well be spent on other things. We live right across the street from a brand new public school, but our kids have to take the bus and go two and a half miles to the parochial school. My oldest daughter doesn't like parochial school, but her mother won't let her change. We fight about this a lot. What can I do?"

I informed the gentleman from Elmira that there was nothing he could or should do now. He made his decision when he married and he must keep his word.

The following excerpts from my mail demonstrate the wide range of interfaith marriage problems:

"I'm a Christian girl who married a Jew. His parents are cold to me. I feel like an outsider."

"I'm a Jew who married a Christian girl. Her parents are cold to me. I feel like an outsider."

"My mother is a Catholic and my Dad is a Baptist. I was brought up as a Catholic. I've studied all religions and the Unitarian Church makes the most sense to me. I am seventeen and feel I should be allowed to choose my own religion. Both my parents are furious with me."

"I'm a Presbyterian who married a devout member of the Church of the Latter Day Saints. She won't allow cigarettes, liquors, or coffee in the house. When we were going together, I thought she'd loosen up, but she got worse. I'm ready to walk out."

"I'm a Norwegian blonde who married a Mexican. Mexicans are Caucasians according to anthropologists, but not according to my father. The way he treats my husband you'd think I married outside my race or something. We are both miserable."

"I'm Abie's Irish Rose, only my marriage isn't turning out like the play. My mother-in-law brings her own dish and silverware when she comes to our house for dinner. I buy kosher meat, but she won't eat it because it wasn't cooked in a kosher pan. If this isn't nuts, what is? When my husband sticks up for her, I could brain him."

"My parents go to different churches. On my sixteenth birthday (and it comes up next week) I'm supposed to decide which faith to choose. I'm so mixed up I could die. My father talks to me privately about his faith and my mother tries to sell me on hers. I've gone to both churches and can't make up my mind. My mother has hinted if I choose my father's church she is through with me. My father has said almost the same thing. What can I do?"

Freedom to worship as we choose is a root element of our society. This principle embraces the freedom to choose a lifetime partner. I nonetheless urge those who ask my advice to select someone of their own race and religious faith. All the evidence gathered by marriage counselling services, all the sociological studies, the divorce statistics and the pronouncements of clergymen of every faith demonstrate that marriages between individuals who share the same religious beliefs stand a better chance of succeeding than mixed marriages.

If you are hopelessly in love with someone of another faith and, knowing the odds are against it, still wish to try for a successful marriage, take heart—you may be the exception that proves the rule.

To sum up

1. The more you have in common with the one you choose, the better your chance for a successful marriage. This means religious training, cultural, social, and financial background. The old saying "opposites attract" may be true in the field of electromagnetics, but it seldom works out in choosing a lifetime partner.

2. Don't marry on the spur of the moment. If love is real, it will last. The tired line "marry in haste, repent at leisure" may be a cliché, but it still makes good sense.

3. Don't marry a person whose chief attraction is sexual. A marriage based on sex will fall apart when the passions cool.

4. Don't marry with the intention of changing your beloved to meet your specifications. It won't work. If during

courtship a person is unfaithful, a heavy drinker, a gambler, or abusive, marriage will not provide the magic cure.

5. Choose someone who wants the same things from life that you want. Discuss in detail your aims, goals, and objectives. Marriage should mean companionship and building a life together.

6. Approach marriage as a permanent relationship and not as an experiment which can be tossed aside if it doesn't work. Marriage is a sacred promise made before God and man—it's a lifetime contract till death do you part.

FOUR

How important is sex in marriage?

*". . . they were both naked, the man
and his wife—and they were not ashamed."*

Genesis 2:25

MORE DIVORCES START in the bedroom than in any
other room in the house. And this is only part of
the story. Millions of married couples who present a
picture of contentment to the outside world have un-
satisfactory sex relations, or none at all.

Judging by my mail, the number one problem in America today is the man and wife problem; more married people write to me about sex difficulties than any other subject. Timid women and shy men will write to a newspaper
columnist for help because it provides the protection of
anonymity. They will put on paper words they could never
speak. I receive thousands of letters which start much the

same as this one from a woman who lives in Scarsdale, New York:

> "I can't talk to my doctor about this because he's a close family friend. Our clergyman is married to my aunt, so he's out. I probably wouldn't have the nerve to discuss this with anyone who knows me anyway. You are my only hope. My husband hasn't touched me in five months. . . ."

In this presumably enlightened era, there is a shocking degree of ambivalence (and just plain ignorance) about what sex really should mean. In an unhealthy way the subject of sex has been overworked on the screen, on the stage and on TV and radio. The glamour of "sex appeal" screams at us from the billboards. Sex sells soap, perfume, coffee, automobiles, mattresses, beer, mouth wash, hair tonic, deodorants and cigarettes. The big idea is to be "desirable" so someone will "love" you.

So what's wrong with being wanted and loved? Nothing. But sex and love are not one and the same. Our Madison Avenue, sex-oriented culture is producing thirteen-year-olds whose imaginations are seven years ahead of their emotional development. The relentless barrage of provocative pictures and slogans, the silken promises, all create premature desires in adolescents. Young people are unable to make any distinction between love and sex. And small wonder, a great many adults have the same problem.

There are some who say too much has been written about sex already and that the best way to put sex in perspective is to play it down or ignore it. Ignoring a problem or sweeping it under the rug will not dispose of it. Others insist that because sex is "natural," a married couple will catch on without any coaching from the sidelines. And this last is a dangerous over-simplification. Two people who have been reared with healthy sex attitudes will surely have an easier time, but no couple should marry with the naive notion that nature will favor them with a harmonious sex life.

Americans today are more frank and articulate about sex than their grandparents were. We hear words like "libido" and "heterosexual" at study groups and cocktail parties. Some bartenders sound like psychiatrists. Almost everyone talks the vernacular. But bandying the words about doesn't mean we are able to relate them effectively to our personal lives. Possession of knowledge doesn't insure that we will be able to apply it. It's not what we know, but what we are able to do with what we know that counts.

All of us are acquainted with physicians who warn their patients against over-eating, and excessive drinking and smoking. Yet often they themselves are dangerously over-weight, they drink too much and smoke three packs of cigarettes a day.

Dr. Allan Fromme points out in his book *The Psychologist Looks at Sex and Marriage* that the formula for a wholesome sex life is really quite simple. He says:

"In order to enjoy sex all we need is the right attitude toward it; namely an unadulterated appreciation, or favorable opinion, of it."

In this chapter I intend to discuss the sex problems about which most married people write me. For every thousand who write, there are many many more thousands who want to know the answers.

We shape our attitudes toward sex at an early age and we are influenced chiefly by our parents. The manner in which parents react to our childish curiosity about the "difference between boys and girls" is what gives us our first inkling. From the beginning, most children are given the vague notion that something is "wrong" with sex. When youngsters are caught "playing doctor" (which they all do, as a method of exploring) they are usually punished and told such things are "nasty" and "bad."

Recently I was visiting in the home of friends who I considered enlightened. Their two-year-old son suddenly appeared in the living room at 11:30 p.m. without a stitch of clothing. The mother was horrified, the father was speechless. Finally he shouted:

"You're a bad boy to come out before company with no clothes on." And then in a taunting, childish tone, the father added:

"Shame, shame double shame—everybody knows your name."

And so it was with most of us. Before we learned anything useful about the human body, we were made to feel there was something wrong with it. It's difficult to go back and unlearn what we have learned. And it is pointless to blame our parents for rearing us with warped ideas. They did the best they could. This was the way *they* were brought up. And, if it's any comfort, this is the way 95 per cent of the children in America were brought up 35 years ago.

The frigid, frustrated, disappointed and unfulfilled who write for help with sex problems range from sixteen to eighty-four years of age. They are bootblacks and bankers, barmaids and Boston Back Bay society matrons. Some who write are unbelievably ignorant and they express themselves in gutter talk because it's the only language they know. Others use terms so technical I've had to send the letters to physicians for translation. These thousands of unhappy people share a common problem—sex.

One day's mail produced the following:

> "Hazel acts as if she's doing me a favor. I practically have to beg her. She has more headaches than any woman who ever lived."

"Jack never puts his arms around me unless he wants something. He's so matter-of-fact about sex, it's disgusting. He makes me feel like a prostitute."

"When Ruth wants an expensive trinket, she bribes me. I'm sick and tired of paying for her favors. She comes from a socially prominent New England family. I can't understand where she learned such ideas."

"Harvey is after me all the time. I can't even take off my stockings in his presence. There must be something wrong with him. Maybe he's a sex maniac."

"Paul and I are both forty-four. I'm too young to dry up. Last year he told me we're getting too old for 'that stuff' and to forget it. He's afraid he'll have a heart attack."

"I'm married to a chunk of ice. I told Mary a year ago if she didn't warm up, I'd find someone who would. She said 'Go ahead. I don't care what you do so long as you don't bother me.' "

Sex attitudes represented in each of these situations resulted from childhood training. If a girl grows up believing that sex is vulgar and nasty or a nuisance that women must tolerate because men like it, she will not suddenly believe it is beautiful and meaningful simply because a clergyman says a few words and hands her a document making it legal.

Our culture insists on female chastity. "Nice girls don't do such things" is drummed into the heads of young girls. Sex is forbidden. Then, suddenly she is a married woman and she's expected, automatically, to abandon her inhibitions and give herself freely, with no feelings of guilt.

Perhaps the most useful single idea to underline is this: *sexual desires are normal and natural.* We are born with sex drives just as we are born with the instinct to satisfy hunger or thirst. Sex is part of a divine plan. God made the sex act the most pleasurable and wondrous of all human experiences to insure the propagation of the species.

If sexual relations in marriage produce strong feelings of guilt, shame, or fear—feelings which interfere with a satisfactory physical relationship—you need professional help to rid yourself of these crippling emotions. Depending on the nature of the problem, it may take four visits with a marriage counselor, three visits with a clergyman, two visits with the family doctor, or four years with a psychiatrist. The important thing is to get help. If you broke your leg, would you go to an orthopedist or would you limp along forever on one leg? With the help available today, it is senseless to go through life hobbled by sick ideas.

Some are cold but few are frozen

The frigid woman is the special target of dissatisfied husbands. Most men who complain about the sexual aspect of their marriage sound like Mr. X., who wrote from a small town in Wisconsin:

> "She's a chunk of ice—just plain cold. When we were going together, I couldn't get to first base. I thought it was because she was so refined and had such high standards. Now I know she's just a cold tomato."

Women who get no pleasure from sexual relations should see a gynecologist to determine if the cause is organic. Although the chances are slim, it is possible a woman's lack of interest is due to a thyroid condition or a pituitary gland that isn't functioning properly.

In most cases, however, the problem is psychological and not physical. The frigid woman usually has a low opinion of sex, is afraid of it or feels guilty about it. Young girls who were trained from early childhood to beware of men and their "evil ways" look upon sex with disgust. After years of fighting off the advances of men, it is difficult to relax and enjoy it. Most frigid women inherited this miserable legacy from a parent who equated sex with sin. Such a twisted idea makes it impossible to find pleasure in marital relations.

Problems involving female frigidity often are rooted in the early relationship with the father. A girl who feared and hated her father in childhood may identify all males with him and be unable to have a mature love for any man. An unusually close relationship between a father and daughter can, on the other hand, produce the same unhappy result. The father-adoring woman may unconsciously substitute her husband for her father, and this incestuous feeling can freeze her totally. Professional help is needed to enable her to perform properly as a wife and love-partner.

No woman (or man) is "born cold." And it is an old wives' tale that Negroes are "hot-blooded" and Scandinavians are "cold-blooded." Sexual activity is regulated by glandular functions which are common to humans of all races, and by emotional conditioning, which is a matter of early training and environment.

Occasionally a woman who has been branded frigid by her husband will write and tell me that her coldness can be traced to the ignorance of a selfish spouse. A Pittsburgh secretary wrote:

> "My mother was a warm and affectionate woman who loved life. I was the same way until I married Grant. He was demanding, inconsiderate and so brutal in his lovemaking that I grew to hate it."

I advised this girl to insist that Grant go with her to a marriage counselor. Talking out the problem with an expert in the field can do wonders. Often a man is unaware that his wife is "cold' because she resents his approach. The woman who feels she is being assaulted is not about to find beauty and satisfaction in the sex act.

A reader from Wichita wrote:

> "My husband says I'm a cold fish, and maybe I am, but how can I be otherwise? Sex to him is about as romantic as a sneeze. When he's through, he's through. No word of love, no pat of tenderness, no sign of warmth or affection. Two minutes later he's snoring his head off."

Earlier in this chapter I said that most men who write to me complain about cold-tomato wives. Do you know what the majority of women write about? They want to know what is "respectable" in married love. "Are there any moral limits?" they ask. I have consulted with clergymen of all faiths, physicians, psychiatrists and psychologists. They all agree that there is nothing indecent or unnatural in married love, provided it is agreeable to both parties and provided there are no harmful or painful effects. Sexual activity is the most private and intimate of all human relationships. It is the language of love. Married couples should feel free to express themselves as they please.

A woman from Kalamazoo wrote:

> "I think I married a nut. He insists on making love with the lights on. He says I'm the one who is off my rocker. How about this?"

I explained to Kalamazoo that neither of them is necessarily a nut, but that her husband's attitude toward sex is probably healthier than hers. I suggested that her false modesty probably covers feelings of guilt. She considers sex something that should be hidden, and darkness is best for hiding. This does not mean that love-making should be conducted under kleig lights, but the lighting or lack of it should be a matter of mature choice. The decision should not be dictated by guilt or unresolved childhood inhibitions.

I urge married couples to tell one another if something bothers them in their love-making. I'm astonished by the number of married couples who tolerate unhappiness in martyred silence when one sentence or two could eliminate the problem. Remember, you married a human being, not a mind-reader. If something is annoying or unpleasant, say so.

A young bride from Youngstown, Ohio, wrote that when her husband became amorous, he insisted on blowing into her ear. "I'm sure he saw this done in the movies and thinks it's a great technique, but it just drives me nuts! I hate it."

I sent the woman a telegram saying, "Just tell him to stop it." She replied in an air mail, special delivery letter the following day: "I took your advice. My husband asked me why I hadn't mentioned it before. He thought I liked it. I guess I was afraid of hurting his feelings, but now I see how foolish I was."

A Philadelphia accountant wrote that his wife was an attractive and desirable woman; he said:

> "We've been married seven years and something has bothered me from the beginning. She has a habit of plumping up the pillows on the bed when we are in a romantic mood. My mother used to do this when I was sick, and it reminds me of her. When I think about my mother, I can't think of sex. It has caused a lot of trouble. I'm afraid to mention this to my wife for fear she'll think I'm crazy. How can I overcome this mental hazard?"

I advised the young accountant that he would probably never be able to overcome completely the mental hazard. So long as he lived, every time a pillow was plumped under his head he would be reminded of his mother. I suggested that he simply throw the pillows out of the bed before his wife could get at them.

A month later I received a letter from a Philadelphia woman. She said:

> "I cannot give you my name and address, but please answer me in the confidential part of your column. Call me 'Baffled.' My husband is an accountant. We've been married seven years and have had some trouble adjusting to each other sexually, but I guess this is natural. About three weeks ago my husband started tossing the pillows out of bed. Since then our sex life has greatly improved. Have you ever heard of this before? What possible effect could this have?"

I replied to "Baffled": "He has decided he doesn't like pillows. If it works, it's good. Forget it."

I cannot overemphasize the importance of open discussion. A man in Los Angeles wrote to thank me for encouraging him to ask his wife why she was unresponsive and often did her laundry at night to avoid going to bed with him.

"I thought my bedroom approach was manly and that I was in complete command of the situation," he wrote, "but after talking it out with Marie, I discovered that she considered me much too rough—anything but romantic."

Some women, on the other hand, prefer a man who is aggressive, decisive, even demanding. A husband who is "too courteous" in his love-making offers little physical satisfaction to a woman who wants to be dominated. Sex is a complicated and sensitive method of communication. It must be learned through practice and this is best accomplished when two partners help one another. Beginners are bound to be clumsy in love-making. Perfection requires time, patience, and mutual guidance.

I've received letters from young brides who were deeply disappointed in the honeymoon.

> "It wasn't at all what I expected," complained a twenty-year-old. "We left the wedding reception at midnight and drove 150 miles. By the time we arrived at the hotel, we were both so tired we couldn't see straight. I had always dreamed that my wedding night would be the most glorious night of my life. Instead it was a nightmare."

This couple (and many others in similar circumstances) were influenced by all the romantic novels they had read and all the Grade-B movies they had seen. How much wiser to have spent the night in a local hotel, or—if they were determined to drive off amid a shower of rice and old shoes—they should have gotten a good night's sleep after reaching their destination.

Men have fewer psychological sex problems than females, but when they occur they are devastating. The inability to perform sexually is called impotence. It is humiliating because the husband is afraid he lacks masculinity. Many men fear there is something "wrong" with them when impotence occurs, and obviously the first step to remedial action is consultation with a physician to determine whether there is an organic disturbance. The chances are one hundred to one, however, that the problem is emotional and not physical.

Impotent (and ignorant) men are a favorite target for quacks. Readers frequently send me ads clipped from cheap magazines which promise the return of vigor and "youth" for two dollars, postage prepaid. I have written hundreds of letters to men advising them that the "love potions" and "nature-restoring creams" are useless and to spend their money instead on professional help.

In the majority of cases impotence is the result of guilt, a conflict between what he feels is right and wrong. In our society (say what you will) the male is not likely to be chaste and virginal until marriage. His mother, father or clergyman may hint strongly, or even demand that he "behave himself," but the fact is that most high school boys have had sexual relations by the time they are seniors.

A young man who has had strict upbringing often hesitates to experiment with girls in his own social crowd. Furthermore he may hear the older fellows say that sexual relations are easier to come by if he selects a girl who doesn't know him. So he may prowl around in a car and pick up a girl off the street or in a tavern, or he may get a phone number from a buddy who has assured him it will be "easy."

A sexual experience with such girls has nothing to do with love or affection. It is purely a matter-of-fact measure to obtain physical satisfaction. The boy's interest is centered on his own pleasure and he couldn't care less about the girl's feelings, or if indeed, she has any feelings at all. He thinks of a girl as something to be used, then cast aside. Some young men who grow impatient with the chase decide it is easier to go to a house of prostitution. They rationalize that it is more convenient to pay a fee and avoid the trouble of putting on a sales pitch. Buying sex is also insurance against rejection.

Yet when these same young men marry, they are expected to regard sexual relations as an expression of love, something beautiful and tender. They are expected to be considerate, loving, and patient. This is a tall order. Attitudes and patterns established in childhood and adolescence are sometimes impossible to discard. A young man who had been married only a few weeks wrote me this letter:

"My wife and I are fighting about—of all things—bedroom wallpaper. This may sound strange to you, but there is a great deal more involved than she realizes. Maybe you can help. We've been married less than two months and are very much in love. I am twenty-two—Charlotte is twenty.

"We rented this old apartment which is cozy, but it needs fixing up. Right now we're selecting wallpaper. Charlotte wants a plain stripe in our bedroom, but I must have a flowered design.

"You'll probably think I'm a loon, but I need help so I'll tell you the whole truth. Before I met Charlotte I had a girl friend I used to see for sex purposes only. She was older than I, and divorced. I never treated her as a date— she was just someone I went to see when I felt the urge. This girl was quiet, uneducated and dull, but sexually she was terrific. She was the first girl I had successfully gone all the way with and I formed quite a strong attachment to her. She lived in a cheap apartment, with flowered wallpaper.

"The first three nights of our honeymoon Charlotte and I slept in a hotel room that had painted walls. I had a terrible time. As soon as we got to our own little apartment with flowered wallpaper in the bedroom, everything was fine. Now Charlotte wants to change the bedroom paper to a stripe. What can I do? I can't tell her the truth. She wouldn't understand. Please rush your advice, General Delivery. I can't take a chance on getting your letter at home.

Mr. E.J.K."

I told the young man to insist that his wife let him have his way. I even suggested dialogue:

"Honey, you can decorate the rest of the place any way you like, but please let me win this one. I may be goofy, but I sleep better in a bedroom that has flowered wallpaper."

Weeks later I received a note from the young man. It was written on flowered wallpaper. He scribbled in crayon:

> "*Dear Ann Landers:* Thank you more than words can express.
>
> E.J.K."

Unfulfilled sexual desires can produce sharp personality changes. The tension created by frustration can make a man unpleasant and vengeful. He may get even with his wife by being tight with money, or mean to her mother, or he may belittle her before guests the next evening. The woman who is left dangling sexually may strike back at her husband by being extravagant with money or hypercritical of his manners.

Couples who find no satisfaction in the bedroom are inclined to fight in the living room, on the back porch, in the kitchen and in other people's homes as well.

Generally speaking, a man who has a satisfactory physical relationship with his wife will not slip his collar and seek extra-marital affairs. There are exceptions, however, and I hear from thousands of wives who are married to them. A woman from Temple, Texas, put it this way:

> "I have made it a rule never to refuse my husband no matter how tired I am. He says I satisfy him completely and that he loves me more today than when we married twenty years ago. Yet every few weeks he comes home with lipstick on his shirt, and loaded. I know he's been with another woman. I can't understand it."

The sad truth is that some men have an immature approach to sex and it is beyond the power of faithful, loving wives to change them. Sexual promiscuity is often a symptom of competitiveness and feelings of inferiority. Some men view the number of conquered females in the same light as a bowler who strives to knock down as many pins as possible. He registers the magic number on an emotional scoreboard. Sex, to him, is an ego-boosting game. Psychiatrists tell us that such "lady-lovers" are not lovers of ladies at all. On the contrary, they have a low regard for women and the conquest of a woman is their way of destroying "the enemy."

Then there is the other Don Juan type who wanders from bedroom to bedroom because he is unsure of his masculinity. He keeps trying to prove to himself that he is capable as well as desirable, by seducing as many women as possible.

Another type of rover boy is the husband whose early sex education was acquired in the back alley. He thinks of sex as vulgar and dirty and cannot get complete satisfaction from his wife who is clean and decent. A legitimate sex object inhibits him because he feels he is defiling a good woman. He can react freely and without inhibition only with a tramp type.

Professional help is the only hope for these sick men, and it is often difficult, if not impossible, to get them to seek the help they need since they see nothing wrong in their behavior. They rationalize their promiscuity by insisting that men are polygamous by nature. To them fidelity is "old fashioned."

Sexual activity requires energy. A man who works 14 hours a day will have less sex drive than the one who bursts into the house every evening at 5:40 p.m. Business pressures can rob a man of his vitality and reduce his sexual appetite. In every normal life there are bound to be periods of anxiety, tension, and overwork; a wife must expect this—and understand it. But the man who becomes a slave to his business and works so hard and long that there is no energy left for loving his wife makes a bad bargain. Often he works and worries himself into an early grave and his wife enjoys the fruits of his labors and the sexual companionship he denied her—with a second husband.

Then, too, the wife who has several small children to police, a large home to clean, plus the laundry and cooking to do, cannot be expected to make like Cleopatra six nights a week. But when a wife finds herself saying "no" more often than "yes," she'd better get smart and hire some help, or let the waxing and polishing go. There are no medals for the girl with the antiseptic cupboards and the gleaming floors if she falls into bed exhausted every night. The man with the "too tired" wife is easy prey for a bouncy, energetic, unattached female—and the world is full of them.

The old-fashioned concept that the male should be the aggressor and the female the shrinking violet is preposterous. In successful marital relations both should play a positive role. Women who have led sheltered lives are sometimes reluctant to display enthusiasm for sex. They fear their husbands may think they are "cheap" or unladylike.

Sexual appetites vary. A race horse teamed with a plow horse is bound to have problems. When such troubles arise, the only solution is to adapt and adjust. This takes maturity, patience, and understanding.

The woman who repeatedly withholds herself from her husband by manufacturing a fake illness can seriously damage her marriage. But if a woman is truly ill, or if she is honestly fatigued at the end of a hectic day, she should feel free to say no without apology or guilt. *Love-making is a privilege, not a duty.* A sense of mutuality should exist if we are to rise above the animal level.

Both men and women have written to ask when sexual activity in marriage should cease. Physicians and clergymen agree there is no time limit on the expression of physical love. As we enter the twilight of our lives, we have less vigor and energy. But medical histories record sexual activities between couples in their seventies and eighties. And some women have written to say they enjoy sex more after menopause because the fear of pregnancy is no longer present.

A wholesome sexual relationship permits the expression of a variety of moods. Understanding and being able to adjust to moods matures a relationship. It is during these intimate moments that we are most nearly ourselves.

Each of us knows the need to overcome his separateness —"to leave the prison of his aloneness." The sexual act, when it is an expression of unselfish love, helps us to surmount our feelings of isolation and separateness. Two become one. The perfect love experience is more than just a physical union. It is a spiritual and mental union as well. For those very special moments, no one else exists in all the world. It is a way of saying "To me, you are the most important person in the universe."

The poets say perfect physical love is man's closest link to heaven. But perfect physical love is not the private property of the poets, or the rich, or the wise. It belongs to anyone who knows how to love and how to give.

FIVE

How to stay married

"All happy families are alike—but an unhappy family is unhappy after its own fashion."

Tolstoy, Anna Karenina

A SUCCESSFUL MARRIAGE is not a gift, it is an achievement. Only a fool assumes that marriage is a prize to be won and then locked in a glass showcase.

Happiness in marriage does not fly in on angels' wings. It is neither endless bliss nor prolonged excitement; emotions of such intensity cannot be sustained. The physical and emotional machinery of man is not geared for perpetual ecstasy. Sensual pleasures have the fleeting brilliance of a comet; a happy marriage has the tranquillity of a lovely sunset.

A good marriage is more than the absence of war. It is a positive, dynamic, growing thing. It is the mature response to obligations. It is the ability to compromise, to give and take, and to share. All who marry hope it will be permanent, but one marriage out of every three in America winds up in the divorce courts. These statistics suggest that a great many people are unable to tolerate the mate they choose, much less attain a reasonable degree of contentment.

A poor relationship between a man and wife is a peculiar kind of agony, but the most unfortunate victims are their children. Sociological studies indicate that hostile, unmotivated and seriously disturbed children are almost always products of separated, divorced, or warring parents. Solid marriages produce children who have feelings of security and a sense of self-esteem. Unhappy marriages produce threatened, unstable youngsters, ill-equipped to be successful husbands or wives. And so the vicious chain continues. Discontented and maladjusted adults pass on to their children these little-understood feelings of insecurity and rootlessness. Only with outside help are they able to gain insight into their problems and give their children the love and affection *they* were denied in their earlier years.

I do not expect that thousands of married couples (or even one) will rush to overhaul their marriages as a result of reading this chapter. I do hope, however, to plant a thought which may help you to keep your marriage together and put it in perspective. I am told by readers that one of the most useful functions of my column is to reduce the awesome dimensions of personal problems by offering a comparison with the heartache in the house next door. And often readers find that the problem isn't next door at all. It's their very own, or close enough so that the advice fits.

An encouraging attribute of the human animal is his potential for development. All of us can be better than we are and the first step in self-improvement is to recognize the need for change.

Keep the lines of communication open

"*Dear Ann Landers:* My husband doesn't talk to me. He just sits there night after night reading the newspaper or looking at TV. When I ask him a question, he grunts 'un-unh' or 'uh-huh.' Sometimes he doesn't even grunt. All he really needs is a housekeeper and somebody to sleep with him when he feels like it. He can buy both. There are times when I wonder why he got married."

Men write with the same complaint, but their letters are less numerous. Here is an excerpt from a Windsor, Ontario, reader:

"My wife doesn't talk to me unless she has a beef against my family or a complaint about the kids or me. We haven't had a pleasant conversation in years. When we were going together, the evenings were never long enough. We never got it all said. What happened anyway?"

The ability to talk things over is the adhesive agent that cements marriages. The husband and wife who can tell it to each other are not likely to tell it to the judge. Incompatibility is a vague word at best. Usually it is another way of saying "We couldn't talk."

The spoken word is only one means of communication. A wink can be eloquent. A raised eyebrow, a smile, a frown, a pat; they all say something. A great deal has been written and spoken about woman's intuition. While I concede that this may be one of her greatest assets, I am certain some of the magic called intuition is simply the intimate knowledge of a familiar face. Individuals who are observant and able to read subtle facial expressions can learn a great deal without exchanging a word.

Problem areas in marriage are best resolved, however, by the spoken word, and I don't mean verbal assault and battery. There can be useful, honorable—even noble—battles in marriage. And there can be vicious, destructive fighting.

All married couples should learn the art of noble battle as they learn the art of making love. It is forthright but never cruel; it is objective, honest, and confined to the problem under discussion. Most arguments get out of hand because one or both parties depart from the central issue. The wife may drag in something from left field in an effort to wound her husband or to cover up the weakness of her own position.

Good battle is healthy. It clears the air. It allows the other person to know what you are thinking and it brings to marriage the principle of an equal partnership. When a woman writes "I'm afraid to open my mouth. He can't take criticism without flying into a rage," I know there is no communication between the couple and that the poor wife is married to a tyrant.

Meaningless chatter may be an outlet, but it is not communication. Witness this complaint:

> "My wife's family is a gabby bunch. They talk constantly. Sometimes they don't make much sense, but they sure do manage to keep the words going back and forth. My family is quiet. I was brought up not to say anything unless I could improve on silence. My wife doesn't understand this."

The woman who marries a no-talk type ("Yup" is a whole speech) sees it another way. One suburban New York wife wrote:

> "After three hours of not saying one solitary word, I handed Ralph the laundry list and said, 'Please read this to me. I just want to hear your voice.'"

The quality of the conversation is what counts, however, and not the quantity. Some couples talk easily about politics, the neighbors, current books, or assorted trivia. This is useful, but the talking that builds a marriage and keeps it in good repair is the honest, below the surface kind. Conversations that advance real understanding deal with personal feelings. The man and wife who can articulate ideas and feelings which they would not express to anyone else usually have a good marriage.

In every family there are some subjects which should be avoided. A remark critical of a man's mother, sister, or brother can, in some circumstances, set off a small war. The wise wife learns to side-step certain sensitive subjects.

Equally explosive are a husband's frequent references to a former sweetheart. A Louisville woman wrote:

> "I never thought I could do such a thing, but when Bill began to rave for the fiftieth time about his old girl friend's fantastic shape, I hit him with the frying pan."

Here are some choice phrases guaranteed to irritate:

"I'm going to tell you something for your own good."

"I've put off mentioning this because I know how sensitive you are."

"I don't like to make comparisons, dear, but my brother Sam would have done it *this* way."

"I was hoping you'd learn this yourself, but since you haven't I'll have to teach you."

"You aren't going to like what I am about to say, but please pay me the courtesy of hearing me out."

Learning the phrases and subjects to avoid is part of the diplomacy of marriage. And learning to tolerate less-than-fascinating conversation is part of marriage, too. A husband should be able to talk to his wife about business problems (and even brag a little if he wants to) without fearing that she'll yawn in his face. A wife should be able to discuss the events of the day without being made to feel that she is boring her husband to death.

Every married couple should discuss their children and decide together what is best for them. One of the chief reasons many children are able to drive a wedge between parents (thus, playing one off against the other) is because Mom doesn't know where Dad stands and Dad isn't aware that Mom has already said no. To present a united front, parents must keep in close communication and decide family policy in regard to hours, car privileges, and so on. This prevents missed signals, wrangling and misunderstanding.

The united front family insists on loyalty. Clearly, a man and wife should not bicker, quarrel, or criticize one another in the presence of others. Letters from both men and women underline the importance of self-discipline. A wife from Kansas City wrote:

> "He's sweet as pie until we get out in company. It's almost as if he waits for an audience so he can belittle my cooking or make cracks about my weight."

A Honolulu husband said:

> "My wife makes me feel like two cents whenever her family is around. She keeps saying in front of her relatives that someday she hopes to have a few of the nice things her sisters have. Their husbands all make big money and she doesn't let me forget it."

Every social circle has at least one couple notorious for "fighting it out in public." The husband or wife who attempts to humiliate his mate only succeeds in working up sympathy for the victim and an active dislike for himself. Some couples are dropped by their friends because their dreary and incessant arguing makes others uncomfortable.

The summary, then, is this: Accept the fact that there is bound to be conflict in every marriage. Don't be ashamed when you can't agree on everything. It is foolish to pretend conflict doesn't exist. A marriage where there is total agreement needs looking into. Someone is not being honest about his feelings. Constructive, honest talking is essential to a good marriage. If something is on your mind, don't just sit there and build an ulcer. Don't let tensions multiply. Work them out as they come along. *Say something.* But remember to say it privately. And finally—never go to bed mad.

Get outside help

Often a visit with an objective third party is precisely what is needed to get a derailed marriage back on the track. I discourage married couples from taking their problems to relatives. In special instances it may work out, but as a general rule the less said to relatives about family problems, the better.

Marriage counseling services are available in almost every city. Readers who live in small towns should contact the Family Service Bureau or the Y.M.C.A. in the nearest metropolitan city and learn of the available facilities.

The clergyman is another excellent source of help. A reader from Cleveland wrote:

> "Thank you for sending me to my minister. He has opened doors for me that I never knew existed. What a wonderful person he is, Ann! And to think he has been available all these years and I didn't even know it."

And remember, you can always write to Ann Landers.

Marriage and money problems

Comparatively few readers write to me about money problems. Since ours is considered a materialistic society, this is surprising—to me, at least.

Women who write about money usually complain about stingy husbands. The following letter is perhaps extreme, but it makes the point:

"What do you think about a husband who keeps crossing things off the grocery list because he says they aren't necessary? He says 'You don't need to buy laundry bleach. Clothes don't have to be snow white. The kids don't need sweet cookies. Let 'em eat crackers. Why buy shampoo when you can wash your hair with a bar of soap? Floors don't need to be waxed. Just keep 'em clean. Furniture polish is a waste of money. Rub a little harder.' We aren't rich people, but we can afford some of the extras in life. It burns me up that he is so tight with me while he spends money on hunting and fishing equipment, drinks for the boys and card playing. I get no allowance. He handles all the money. I'll have to shake four cents out of the baby's bank to mail this letter. Please tell me what to do. I'm fed up to here."

I tell wives who do write about this problem that unless a woman is addle-brained or alcoholic, she should be able to handle the grocery money without supervision. It is degrading to be followed around in a store and told what to buy. Most wives do a remarkable job of stretching the pay check. I doubt that their husbands could do as well.

As a matter of self respect every wife, if her husband is employed, should have an allowance for herself. She should be free to spend a few dollars a week as she pleases and be accountable to no one.

Policies regarding family finances are best ironed out before marriage. It should be decided in advance who is to handle the money and pay the bills. In some marriages the husband is better qualified. Often, however, it is the wife. A man from Atlanta told me:

"We were broke and in debt the first two years of our marriage. I was handling the money and I couldn't make ends meet. My wife asked for a chance to take over. I figured she couldn't do much worse than I had done, and maybe she could do better. In less than a year she had us out of debt and she had $250 put away in the bank. She certainly surprised me. I take my hat off to her."

The wife who is in charge of the family purse strings should see to it that her husband has enough spending money. It's rough for a man to have to ask his wife for cigarette change or "a couple of dollars to buy gas for the car." The husband who turns his pay check over to his wife should get money to cover his daily expenses, and he should not be expected to account for every dime.

If both husband and wife are working, I recommend that the checks be pooled and the incomes treated as one. A good marriage should be a partnership—spiritual, moral, physical, and financial. There should be no "mine" and "thine"—only "ours."

Accept the realities of marriage

To improve any situation we must all start here and now with what we are and with the resources at our command. There is no turning back the clock or undoing what has been done, unless you are a magician, in which case this chapter is not for you.

Most married people, if they are honest, will admit that marriage isn't all they had hoped it would be. No union between earthly creatures can possibly measure up to the florid promises of the movies, love novels, and advertisements for cedar chests. Married life as we live it is certain to come off second best when compared with our popular romantic fantasies. Somerset Maugham summed it up neatly: "American wives expect to find in their husbands a perfection English women only hope to find in their butlers."

It is essential, then, if we are to enjoy a mature relationship, to accept the realities of married life. It has been said that rose-colored glasses do not come in bifocals because nobody reads the small print in dreams. Examine the small print in the marriage contract; perhaps it will help you to put your own marriage in its proper perspective.

America has the largest middle class in the world. The very rich and the very poor are a small percentage of this country's population. Less than one-tenth of one per cent of American males have an annual income of $10,000 a year or more.

The picture of the average American woman as an over-privileged, pampered house cat is preposterous. It is not the Junior League or the yacht club that consumes the average woman's time and energy. It's a plugged sink, Billy's measles, patching clothes, marketing, cooking, washing and ironing, stretching an inadequate pay check and dragging her husband away from the TV set so he'll pay a little more attention to her.

The following letter from Houston tells the story for thousands of women:

> "The kids are in bed, the dishes are stacked in the sink and there's plenty of mending I could do, but I'm going to let everything sit. Tonight I'm keeping a promise I made to myself a year ago. I'm going to write to Ann Landers.
>
> "Jack and I have been married sixteen years. He had a good education and I always told myself he'd make the grade. Well, he never has—quite. The pay check barely covers the necessities. Our five kids, God bless them, are healthy and smart, but they keep me on the brink of exhaustion.

"If Jack takes me to a movie every couple of weeks, it's a big deal. He's a swell guy, and I do love him, but this isn't exactly what I expected out of life. A meal in a restaurant would be like a dream come true. I'm yearning for just a little bit of real fur on a suit. Tell me, Ann, is this a life?

Jane"

The reply:

"You bet it's a life, Jane, and a darned good one. Did you know that people can get just as exhausted from boredom as from overwork? And sirloin in a restaurant can begin to taste like sawdust after a while, too.

"I've had stacks of letters from women with open charge accounts asking what to do with their lives. And many write about problems that resulted from too much leisure. They sought escape from boredom through alcohol and extra-marital affairs.

"Sure you get fed up, everybody does, but don't lose your perspective. You've got the things that count. Pity the poor millionaire. He'll never know the thrill of paying that final installment."

It is vital to your mental and physical health that you learn to accept your mate as he is. It's a foolish mistake to figure that after marriage you will make him (or her) over to suit your specifications. By the time a man or woman is of marriageable age, the behavior patterns are set.

This is not to say there will be no personality changes, no emotional or intellectual development. Maturity should come with the passing years. As our horizons broaden, we should become less petty, more patient and understanding. The man at forty-four is not what he was at twenty-four. The woman at thirty-eight has grown beyond the notion that the most important goal in life was the presidency of her sorority.

A wise husband or wife can subtly influence his mate and, by example, demonstrate that some approaches to life work better than others. But it won't be achieved by attempting to impose ideas on an unwilling subject or by nagging criticism.

Since marriage is the most intimate and most demanding of all adult relationships, conflict is inevitable. A woman meets a crisis like a woman. She's likely to weep when she's frustrated or angry. A man is more apt to raise his voice and spout forth a stream of verbal complaints or he may clap on his hat and leave the house for a few hours. Try to remember to attack the problem and not each other.

Personal habits can be a source of real trouble. It is my opinion (but many readers have disagreed with me) that a man is neat or he is not neat when you marry him, depending on the training he received from his mother. The next letter is typical of a complaint which has come to me from every state in the union, plus Panama, Puerto Rico, Canada, Nassau and Scotland.

"My husband thinks you are God's gift to the American husband. Me—I would like to wring your neck. Several months ago you said a wife should iron the bed sheets if her husband likes them that way, so I started to iron the bed sheets on your say so. That controversy led to whether a woman should iron her husband's shorts. You said 'if a husband wants his shorts ironed—then iron 'em.' So my big slob, who never knew that shorts could be ironed, showed me the column and said 'Ann thinks you should iron my shorts from now on.'

"I was pretty burned up; in fact I even considered sending you a bundle of my husband's shorts to iron, but I decided to be a good sport and go along with it. Now you come along with the insane advice that a wife should pick up after her husband. If you can tell me why an able-bodied man should get this kind of service, I'll do as you say and never mention it again.

Livid Viv"

I told Livid Viv (and hundreds of other women who bombarded me with invective) that if a woman marries a man who leaves his pajamas on the floor, his ties on the doorknob, and his shorts wherever he happens to drop them, she should pick up after him and say nothing. He was brought up that way and no amount of nagging is likely to change him. Pick up after him not for his sake, but for yours. The time involved can't possibly amount to more than ten minutes a day. Does it make sense to fuss and fume over something so insignificant? Constant "reminding" makes you a nag and you usually wind up picking up after him anyway. Then everybody's mad. It's not worth it.

Perfection is achieved only when one can be in complete control of one's self at all times. This means operating on an even keel, with no sharp peaks and valleys, no moods, no loss of temper, no display of vanity, anxiety, weakness, indecision or despair. If such a person exists, I would like to have him dipped in bronze and put on display in the Smithsonian Institution.

Physical condition has an important bearing on behavior. A woman does not feel the same every day of the month. Neither does a man. The endocrine system, which is the glandular network regulating our energy output, has a direct effect on disposition and personality. All of us operate in cycles. Even in the course of a single day energy peaks vary. The man who could go bear hunting with a switch at eight in the morning may fold like an accordion 12 hours later. His wife may not come alive until noon.

Timing is crucial. The tired husband is likely to be irritable and negative. The moment he walks into the house is not the appropriate time to shove the bills in his face and complain about the children. The woman who has had a particularly trying day is not likely to be fit as a fiddle and ready for love.

In accepting the realities of marriage, try to see the humor in situations which may seem deadly serious at the moment. Laughter offers a healthy release from tension and anxiety. It is an ideal device to head off a big argument or to end a small one. The husband who wrote that his wife burns him up because she squeezes the toothpaste tube from the middle had no sense of humor, and less imagination. (Being a middle-squeezer myself I know it's a habit which was acquired early.) The man who is so exacting that he can't tolerate a tube squeezed from the middle should develop a sense of humor for the sake of his blood pressure.

Finally

Think of your marriage in terms of what's right with it rather than what's wrong with it. If you can look at a bottle and say "it's half full" rather than "it's half empty" your approach is positive, and this philosophy will help make a marriage work. Think in terms of "we" and "us" rather than "me" and "I."

Don't envy your neighbor because his or her marriage may look more exciting or glamourous. You never know what's going on behind closed doors and drawn drapes. They may be envying you. The only home life about which you will ever know the whole truth is your own. Broaden your perspective and measure the good aspects of your marriage against the bad. Then, when the sledding gets a little bumpy (and you can be sure it will), remember that wonderful old Yiddish adage "Ahless in ainem nish-taw bah kainem," which means in any language "Everything in one person—nobody's got it."

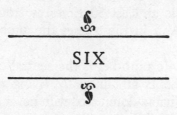

SIX

Must we outlaw the in-law?

"Wherefore shall a man leave his father
and mother, and shall cleave to his wife: and they
shall be two in one flesh."   Genesis 2:24

T HE ONLY SURE WAY to avoid in-law trouble," said a
latter-day wit, "is to marry an orphan."

How serious is the in-law problem? Has it been exag-
gerated? Has the American mother-in-law earned her black
eye or is she the innocent victim of gag-writers?

My mail provides daily evidence that the in-law problem
is no myth. Experts say in-laws figure in three out of every
five divorces. Is it any wonder the cry "outlaw the in-law"
is heard throughout the land!

Our social critics say the American matriarchy has
shunted Dad so far into the background that he isn't even
important enough to make trouble. This may be more than

a lame joke. The evidence I've seen indicates that the mother-in-law is at least 50 times as troublesome as the father-in-law. And in most cases the problem is the husband's mother.

When the wife's mother is the central cause for marital discord, it presents an unusually trying problem for the husband. The mama-dominated wife never gets over feeling like a naughty child when she goes against her mother's wishes, or heaven forbid, when she puts her husband first.

The most troublesome relative, after the mother-in-law (his or hers) is the sister-in-law (usually *his* sister). The brother-in-law is close on her heels and the father-in-law comes straggling in a poor fourth.

An Indiana attorney wrote:

> "I've been practicing law for over 15 years and have handled hundreds of divorce cases. I do not approve of divorce and I try to effect a reconciliation whenever possible. It is my opinion that two-thirds of all divorces can be traced directly to in-law trouble. Not only are parents at fault, but grandparents, brothers, sisters and even shirt-tail relatives are often responsible for broken marriages.
> "If in-laws would make it their business to mind their own business, the divorce courts would not be so crowded."

The threadbare phrase "I'm marrying *him* (or her), not the whole family," is unrealistic. In rare instances it is possible to steer clear of all relatives. But generally, even if physical separation is accomplished, it is difficult to sever the emotional bonds. Family ties are like roots, and roots lie buried beneath the surface.

The mother who won't let go of her son

One of the singular aspects of the mother-in-law problem is that wives thousands of miles apart use almost identical language to describe it. The letter that follows came from a small town in Connecticut. It might have come from any one of hundreds of cities where my column appears.

> "My mother-in-law's interference is ruining my marriage. She bosses my husband as if he were a child. When he takes her side, I want to walk out of the house and never come back. I don't know how much longer I can take it."

This, of course, is the way the daughter-in-law sees it, and she could be justified. It may be, however, that she is too sensitive or overly critical. I have suggested to thousands of couples who are plagued with in-law troubles that they visit a marriage counselor or a clergyman and verbalize their feelings. An unbiased third party, trained in handling family problems, may give them both a fresh look at the other side.

The daughter-in-law is often unaware of the problems of a mother of three or four adult children who suddenly finds herself with an empty nest. For the past twenty years she has been busy with her children and then, one by one, they leave her. Her interests are frequently limited to a club or church group. Life becomes frighteningly empty and sterile. She has nothing important or demanding to occupy her time and energy, so she turns to "helping" her newly-married children. She means well, but a young bride who wants to work things out in her own way may consider it meddling.

When mother-in-law offers suggestions to Betty on what to do about Ted's cold (after all, who knows better than a boy's mother?) Betty interprets it as "butting in." A marriage counselor or a clergyman can point out that a mother's interest in her son is normal and that a mother-in-law can be useful to a daughter-in-law who is willing to accept gracefully a few well-intentioned suggestions.

This next letter from Virginia illustrates a problem which is more complex because it involves two gravely neurotic people—a mother and her son:

> "My mother-in-law is making a nervous wreck out of me. She lives in an apartment about two miles from us (the closest one she could find) and my husband is her sole means of support. Her medicine bills and doctors cost us a fortune. She takes pills to go to sleep, to wake up, to calm her nerves, balance her thyroid, slow up her breathing and pep up her blood. Three times last week she phoned us in the middle of the night to say she was dying. My husband dragged himself out of bed and rushed to her bedside. She's been pulling this same stunt for ten years. The doctors can find nothing organically wrong with her. She'll probably bury me. I've tried to tell my husband she is a clever woman who fakes illness to get attention. He says she is his mother and whatever she wants him to do, he will do whether it makes sense or not. Can you suggest a course of action for me?
>
> Fed to the Teeth"

The wife who is trapped in such a situation has a rough life. Her best hope is to persuade her husband to seek psychiatric treatment so that one day he may detach himself from his domineering and demanding mother. A grown man who says, "Whatever my mother wants me to do I will do whether it makes sense or not" concedes that he is operating at an infantile level.

If the mother-in-law is unbearably punishing, I advise the wife to tell Junior to go live with Mama until he grows up, and I suggest that she remind him to send the support checks in the mail.

The most difficult of all the mother-in-law problems in-

volves the only son of a widowed or divorced woman.
Young men who grow up with no male influence in the
home are often poor marriage risks. There are exceptions,
of course, but the evidence is heavily weighted on the negative side.

Some months ago, I received the following letter from a
North Carolina bride:

> "I am writing this letter on my wedding night. My
> groom and I were married this afternoon in a beautiful
> church ceremony. We left the hotel reception at about
> eight-thirty in the evening and drove to this lovely little
> resort hotel. The first thing my husband did when we
> arrived here was telephone his mother. They talked for
> thirty minutes and he spent most of the time comforting
> her and trying to get her to stop crying. After the con-
> versation he flopped down on the bed, bawled for ten
> minutes, cracked open a pint of bourbon, drank it and
> passed out."

Her signature, several pages later, was "Unmarried Wife."
If you think such neurotic relationships exist only between mother and son, please read the next letter. This
problem occurs less frequently. But it does happen.

> "Our son went steady with a lovely girl for two years.
> The girl's father died when she was thirteen and she and
> her mother were like sisters. We knew they were close,
> but we didn't realize they were crazy. We should have
> known something was wrong when the mother moved to
> the college town and took a selling job to be near her
> daughter. After graduation B and J had a nice wedding.
> On the wedding night J complained of a sick headache.
> The next day she said her eyes hurt. That night her back
> ached. The next morning she scribbled a note saying she
> couldn't bear to think of her mother alone so she had
> taken the bus home. What can our son do?
>
> Shocked Parents"

Again, psychiatric help is the only solution. But too often, as I told this woman, professional help is rejected. The sick ones defend their behavior with such fancy (and even admirable) labels as "mother love," "family devotion" and "filial loyalty." When I advised a New York reader to get outside help before his mother's apron strings throttled his marriage, he replied:

> "There is nothing wrong with me, Ann Landers. You are the one who needs professional help. My wife is twenty-eight years old. She has her whole life before her. My mother is sixty-four. I shall continue to spend every January in Florida with my mother as long as she lives. My wife belongs home with the children."

Competition between the generations

Some women dislike their mothers-in-law even before they meet and it's the husband's fault. He sometimes paints such glowing pictures of "dear old mom" that he gives the girl an inferiority complex, and plants a premature dislike for this paragon in-law.

Many mother-in-law problems are bound up in some way with food, perhaps because food is an ancient symbol for love. It may be the unconscious motivation for two women who attempt to battle it out in the kitchen.

These complaints tell the story: "My husband's mother phones him at work and asks him to stop by her house for his favorite dish—meatballs and cabbage." Or, "My mother-in-law insists on bringing matzo-ball soup over here because she knows Lou loves it, and I can't make it as well as she can." A woman who had been married seven years wrote, "My mother-in-law comes over every Wednesday and takes over my kitchen. She likes to prepare special Italian dishes for her son. I've asked her for recipes dozens of times, but she claims she never measures anything."

I tell these wives they can only win by cooperating. If a mother-in-law wants to prepare special dishes and bring them over—fine. If she wants to come to the house once a week and cook a meal, what's wrong with that? Many women are happy to pay a caterer a good price to do the same thing. If a mother-in-law finds pleasure in doing these things for her son, why fly into a rage? The smart wife who permits her mother-in-law the satisfaction of mixing batter in her kitchen now and then often insures that her mother-in-law will not mix in more vital matters.

When I was a bride of twenty-one, my husband let me know that he loved eggplant Romanian style, the way his mother made it. On my first trip to Detroit, some months later, I asked my mother-in-law to show me how to prepare the dish. Step number one was burning the vegetable over the open flame on a gas stove. Step number two—add a raw onion and chop the eggplant and onion together for twenty minutes. I knew then and there I would never make the grade because I loathe chopping onions. After many failures with this miserable vegetable I decided to let my mother-in-law have the title of Eggplant Queen. Whenever my husband goes to Detroit, he stops at his mother's to indulge in a huge bowl of Romanian eggplant. She enjoys every tear shed over that wooden chopping bowl, he gets eggplant up to his ears, and everybody's happy.

Newlyweds should live alone

Newlyweds will be happier in a one-room apartment, even if it's under a bowling alley, than in a mansion which belongs to parents. Every young couple should be free to settle its differences privately, outside the hearing range of relatives. They should have a place of their own in which to make the transition from cloud nine to down-to-earth living.

No two women make a bed or peel a potato exactly the same way. The mother-in-law may make a better apple pie, but even if it isn't better, her son will probably think it is because he grew up on it. Because of the natural competition between a man's wife and his mother, stage settings for conflict should be kept to a minimum. Living under one roof is bound to produce a long list of small irritations. And an accumulation of irritations can add up to an atomic explosion after several months.

Newlyweds often have difficulty adjusting sexually. In-laws in an adjoining bedroom can complicate the problem. Young marrieds are frequently shy and the knowledge that parents are close by can be horribly inhibiting.

One young bride wrote from Salt Lake City:

> "We moved into my mother-in-law's home because she begged us to. She said she would be lonely by herself in that big house, and explained that it would give us a chance to save some money until Jack got on his feet. After the first week I knew it was a foolish move. Our sex life was awful. His mother always managed to knock on our door at the wrong time."

Who should come first, the wife or the husband's mother?

If I could hand every newly married couple a framed motto as a wedding gift, it would say this: "Your first allegiance is to each other. Let no man or woman come between you." No, I am not suggesting that the parents of newly married couples should join the foreign legion. My motto, however, would spare millions of young people the agony of split loyalties.

The man who is unwilling to put his wife before his

mother is not sufficiently mature for marriage. The woman who is unable to put her husband before her parents is not sufficiently grown up to be a wife.

A young wife wrote that just as she was going into labor her husband left her to drive his mother to a bridge party. I knew that short of a miracle she would feel forever second to her mother-in-law. The humiliated woman wrote: "I had to phone the neighbor next door to drive me to the hospital. I'll never get over the shame."

Realigning loyalties can be agonizing, particularly when a parent is involved. Feelings of guilt can play havoc when a choice must be made between two people who are close to us. Sons and daughters who have been reared successfully do not feel that marriage imposes a choice; there are no pangs of guilt attached to leaving mama and papa. The goal for all children should be independence. The successful parent prepares his child to stand on his own and be a central figure in another family. Too often the parent who refuses to let go and insists "my child needs me" is twisting the facts. What he means is "I need my child."

The adult approach is to recognize the different kinds of love. It is possible to love—and at the same time—a wife, a mother, a sister and a grandmother, cherry pie, football, Lincoln, Rembrandt, and Bach. But we don't love them all in the same way. The kind of love which results in marriage should be unique. It should be a combination of admiration, respect, physical desire, mutual interests and mutual goals.

The key to the in-law problem—independence

Some newlyweds as well as long-married couples create their own in-law trouble. They feel free to borrow money, accept large financial gifts, drop in on mom for meals any old time, ask her to baby-sit and present her with their youngsters when they go on trips. If the mother-in-law is used as a sitter because she is handy and free, then the mother should be content to let her unpaid sitter discipline the children in her own way. If the disciplinary methods are not to the young wife's liking, she does not have the right to complain. I frequently receive letters from wives who say:

> "My mother-in-law is ruining our children. When we leave them at her house weekends, they run wild. She gives them candy and ice cream between meals, lets them watch TV until they fall asleep on the floor, and she doesn't even insist that they keep their hair combed and their faces clean."

I tell such women to hire a sitter and give her orders. It's cheaper in the long run and it will save wear and tear on everyone.

Independence from in-laws is vital if young marrieds are to build a solid relationship. A husband and wife should not carry their personal disagreements to the homes of their parents, either individually or together. Husband and wife troubles should be settled between themselves. One wise mother-in-law from San Luis Obispo wrote:

> "When my daughter-in-law and son begin to raise their voices and I see an argument brewing, I leave. I don't want to witness any quarrels. I don't ever want to be asked to take sides."

The wife who tattles on her husband and the husband who down-grades his wife are disloyal. The knowledge that a mate has blabbed about intimate family problems can destroy for all time the trust and confidence which are essential to a sound marriage.

The mature husband and wife run little danger of in-law

interference because they were reared to lead their own lives. Mature people don't get that way by accident. They can make decisions, accept responsibility for themselves, and they don't whine to mom and dad when things go wrong.

In-laws can be wonderful

The Bible story of Naomi and Ruth eloquently describing the devotion between a woman and her daughter-in-law has been repeated millions of times in every country in the world. Many warm and beautiful in-law relationships exist today, as my mail testifies. Often when readers write about unrelated problems, I note the line: "My mother-in-law is a marvelous person. She has helped us in so many ways. I love her dearly."

To all mothers-in-law I would like to say this: If you once had to put up with an interfering mother-in-law, try to remember what it was like. Spare your daughter-in-law the hell you endured. If your mother-in-law was wise and understanding, you know how fortunate you were. Give your daughter-in-law the same break.

Since it is the wife who most often complains to me about her husband's mother, I would like to direct my closing lines to her. Think ahead. One day you will probably be a mother-in-law. You will wish to be treated with kindness and understanding. You won't want to be shut out of the lives of your children. Remember that every mother has an emotional investment in her children. In the evening of her life, her greatest joys and satisfactions come from the knowledge that her children are content and that she is loved by them. When your mother-in-law gets you down and granted, she may be off base a country mile, remember that no one is without some fault. Be tolerant. Be forgiving. Remember, she raised the boy you selected for a husband.

Marriage is not for everyone

THE DIVORCE RATE in America is at an all-time high and it is going up. The bars and taverns are crowded with married men who would rather sit around and get stoned than go home. They spend hours seeing double and acting single. Magazines continue to print helpful articles on "How to Hang on to Your Husband" while the wives write to me and complain that hanging is too good for 'em. And still the cry is heard throughout the land. "You oughta get married."

Our society exerts enormous pressure on both men and women to "get married and live happily ever after." Some employers insist on it; they run advertisements which specifically state "Only married men need apply." The implication is that married men are more reliable than single men. But are they? Well, some are and some aren't.

Relatives often view the unmarried member of the family as the odd one. Parents, grandparents, uncles, aunts, and cousins by the dozen, are forever looking for "a nice girl for Irving." Well-meaning friends never give up trying to put the singleton in double harness. Some singletons need and appreciate a friendly assist but it's a safe bet that when a man or a woman reaches the middle thirties without a trace of rice in his hair, he's better off single.

I don't believe that marriage is good for everyone. Some people should go it alone. I call them non-marriageables and they arrange themselves into distinct categories.

The most obvious non-marriageable personality is the adult who can't cut loose from his family. This apron-string type is most frequently a male. Every community, no matter how small, has at least one. He is attractive, intelligent, successful and considered "very eligible." He often dates a lovely woman for several years and tells all within hearing distance that he'd like to marry her some day, but for all kinds of complicated reasons he must wait. Put all his reasons together and they spell M-O-T-H-E-R.

Pity the woman who falls for him. She finds herself with a pleasant escort, good company, and out of circulation. No other man would ask her for a date because she's spoken for. She is reluctant to break off with him because she's "grown accustomed to his face"—and she keeps telling herself that eventually, when all his problems are solved, they'll be married.

The following letter from Cincinnati illustrates such a situation:

"I've been going with a man for 12 years. I'll call him Ron. He is thirty-eight years old. I am thirty-five. We belong to the same church, we're college graduates and we share common interests. The wedding date has been set five times in the past ten years. Each time he has postponed it. The last three postponements were because of his mother. Ron claims her health is poor and she couldn't stand the excitement.

"I offered to be married in her living room with just the family present. He said no—even that would be too much. Ron lives at home and he's made it clear that when we marry I must move into his mother's house because she could not be left alone. I agreed. In fact I have agreed to everything he has asked for, but still no results. I love Ron and I know he loves me. The years aren't doing me any good. I'm afraid I'll be too old to have a family if we don't get married soon. What can I do?

Not Getting Any Younger"

I told her that 12 years is much too long just to "go with" a fellow and that she should tell him promptly either to fish or cut bait. The man who gets such an ultimatum usually cuts bait, and it's just as well. He doesn't really want to get married. He enjoys the company of women (particularly sex privileges) and to the casual observer he appears to possess all the qualities that make for a fine husband. But he's unwilling to take on the responsibilities of a husband. Marriage frightens him.

The next letter deals with a woman who has the same problem. She is outnumbered by her male counterpart about 100 to 1, judging from the letters I receive, but she does exist. It is her steady boy friend who writes:

"Before I drop this sweetheart of mine right on her smart head I would like a word from you. Frankly, I've just about had it, but if you say to give her a little more time, I will consider it. We've been going together seven years. Kate is thirty-four years old and has never married. I am forty-four and have been divorced ten years. When we first met, I couldn't figure out how a girl with her looks, charm and brains escaped marriage, but I'm beginning to understand.

"She's a newspaper woman, witty, full of pep and stimulating company. She lives with her father who is a doctor. Her mother died when she was a teen-ager. Kate is often expected to attend social functions in connection with her job—cocktail parties honoring celebrities, previews, receptions and so on. She frequently brings her father instead of asking me to accompany her. Then too, she goes to the annual medical convention with her father, which means part of her vacation time is spent with him. I asked her to marry me in the spring and she said her Dad had invited her on a two-month trip to the Far East and she was arranging for a leave of absence. When I told her it was marriage or the trip and she could take her choice, she accused me of pressuring her and asked for more time. What should I do?

Tired of Waiting"

I told "Tired" to give her as much time as she wanted, the rest of her life in fact, but that *he* ought to quit wasting *his* time and find a woman who was grown up enough to get off her Daddy's lap.

Another non-marriageable type is the one whose wife writes to me, unfortunately, following the marriage. He is the incurable skirt-chaser. This letter from Santa Barbara, California, tells the story:

"I've been married for 16 years. We have a lovely family and a beautiful home. If you met us socially you'd think we were a very happy couple. No one knows how much swallowing of pride I've done to keep our home together. We were married less than three months when he began to chase around. First it was a woman in his office. He'd been seeing her during courtship and couldn't get out of the habit. Then it was the nurse who worked the night shift when he had minor surgery. Next, the wife of a young man who worked for him, then a divorcée in our crowd (a good friend of mine). He would admit to each affair when it was over and beg me to forgive him. His latest fling was with a college girl. She is only four years older than our own daughter. This was the most crushing blow of all. I'm at the end of my rope. I find lipstick on his handkerchiefs and telephone numbers in his pockets. Women phone him at home and he says, 'I can't talk now.' I'm not a cold person, Ann, if that's what you're thinking. In fact I never refuse him. He doesn't need to go looking for love. Divorce is out; it's prohibited by our religion. Tell me, please, what can I do?

Don Juan's Wife"

Although it is Mrs. Juan who asks for help, it's her husband who needs it. I explained that she had married a man who should have remained single. He is insecure, doubts his virility, and needs perpetual reassurance. A new conquest is the best prop for his sagging self-esteem. Therapy is sometimes successful, but few men will go to a psychiatrist with the problem because they fail to equate sexual promiscuity with emotional illness. They envision themselves as irresistible lady killers.

Some wives tolerate such shenanigans better than others. If there are children I advise the wife to try to keep the home together. But if a husband's chasing is so flagrant that it brings humiliation and distress to his family, I suggest that the wife invite him to move out of the house. Unfortunately, the chronic rover boys seldom straighten up and fly right. They usually give up the chase only when they wear out.

Now and then a letter will come to me describing the plight of a husband whose wife needs constant attention from a variety of lovers. A man from Harrisburg, Pennsylvania, wrote:

"I worked the night shift and would get home about three in the morning. Whenever I opened the front door I thought I heard the back door slam. For a long time I was sure I was imagining things. Finally I began to hear rumors, so I hired a private detective. In the course of 21 days, my wife entertained eight different men, including the butcher, the real estate agent who sold us our home, an insurance salesman and a couple of close friends of mine."

Obviously, this woman is too sick for marriage. If she hadn't married, she would have spared her husband untold agony.

Then there are those who don't want to marry but don't know it. Their fears are below the conscious level, and they keep the truth well hidden, even from themselves. Men and women populate this category equally. If you suggest that they have no genuine desire to marry, they enter devout and loud denials. But don't believe them. Here's one from Syracuse, New York:

"I'm thirty-three and I've been going with a bachelor for five years. Just when I think everything is set and start to make plans for our wedding, something happens. Harry has a genius for getting himself involved in business deals that keep him broke. The guy is forty-four, handsome, fascinating, nobody's fool, and we like the same things.

"He is also a target for every phony who passes through town. Two years ago, when we had our wedding date set, he got into a deal with some fast operators who imported semi-precious stones. They were guaranteed to look like diamonds only you had to heat them up every six months or they'd get cloudy. He went for his total savings on that one so we had to postpone the wedding plans. Last April I was all set to be a June bride. In May somebody sold Harry a salt mine which belonged to the state of Utah.

He was so broke after that deal that I had to lend him money to live on.

"He says he loves me but he refuses to get married until he can assume the financial responsibilities of a husband. The way things have been going, I'm beginning to think that day will never come. How much longer do you think I will have to wait?"

The answer is obvious: "Probably forever."

Women who drag their feet on the way to the altar employ a variety of devices. The most tired excuse is "I have to take care of 'mama' or 'papa.'" They always seem willing and able to take care of everyone but themselves. A man from Grand Rapids wrote about his woman friend, with whom he'd been going for 11 years. Her device was interesting. He said:

> "I can never get her alone. She has three nieces and two nephews and whenever I go to her place, she has one of them there. She takes them along on dates, asks if I mind, and of course I say no."

I told "Grand Rapids" there must be something wrong with him as well as the woman if he has stood still for this dodge for 11 years. She has been protecting herself against serious involvement by using her nieces and nephews as bodyguards.

Another non-marriageable type is the undeveloped juvenile. The male predominates. Such men were spoiled as children, usually by mama, an auntie or their sisters. They are incapable of loving because loving means giving and they don't know how to give. They need continual flattery, must be catered to, amused and pampered. When they don't get their way they are ill-tempered and sometimes abusive.

Women who marry these selfish little boys bargain for a

lifetime of misery. From Rochester, Minnesota, comes a typical bill of particulars:

> "My purse is so empty I have to stuff tissue paper in it so it won't look flat. When I say my husband doesn't give me a dime, I'm not exaggerating. He pays all the bills and says there is nothing left over. Yet he has one of the best gun collections in the state. Last month he traded his motorcycle for a new one. He has two cycling outfits that cost over $100 apiece. I haven't had a new winter coat in six years. He leaves the children and me five evenings a week to go cycling with his friends. Most of them are teen-agers."

Another example, from Butte, Montana:

> "My husband has left me every weekend in the past three years. He takes off on Friday and doesn't come home until late Sunday night. It's bowling trips, hunting, fishing, skiing, football games, anything that happens to be going on out of town. When I told him I was sick and tired of staying home and that we ought to go out together once in a while, he said, 'Didn't I take you to the hospital in April to have the baby?'"

The most easily recognized non-marriageable female is the wildly competitive type. The poor boob who marries her deserves sympathy instead of congratulations. Everyone (but the victim) seems to know what he's in for. The competitive woman is usually successful in business or a profession. She is competent, aggressive, driven and domineering. Her theme song is "anything you can do, I can do better." She hails the taxi, orders the dinner, finishes his sentences and wants to lead on the dance floor. She is a better man than he is and she lets him know it. She pours a great deal of her energy into her work and finds her major satisfaction in the feeling of importance that it gives her.

She makes a lively dinner companion but a horrible wife. To her a man is an audience, a whipping boy, an object of her hostility and sometimes a willing slave. If she marries, she usually selects a Milquetoast character who is searching for a reincarnation of his bossy and punishing mother.

The non-marriageable men who possess excessively aggressive characteristics are the compulsive workers or the money grabbers. The compulsive worker can be a scientist, a newspaper editor, a politician, or an artist, but usually he's a businessman. He eats, sleeps and dreams his career. It is not money that motivates him; in fact he frequently passes up more lucrative opportunities to stay with the work he loves. He would rather work than eat or sleep and often this is precisely what he does. Such a man is better off single. He contributes little to marriage and it is difficult for any wife to settle for the crumbs.

The money grabber can often fool a woman. She is deluded into thinking he'll make a good husband because he is obviously headed for financial success. He is dynamic, aggressive, indefatigable and imaginative, all fine qualities. But they can be destructive qualities when they're not balanced by a decent set of values. This letter from Washington, D.C., underlines the dangers:

"My husband and I have been married 12 years. I can count on one hand the number of times in the past two years that he has sat down at the dinner table with the children and me. He is either out of town on a big deal or having his dinner with business associates. Oh, he's successful all right—if you measure success by a beautiful home, two cars, a cook, a maid and charge accounts. The best part of my marriage is our three children, and I had to travel with my husband on business trips to get pregnant.

"My friends envy me because we have had fabulous 'vacations' all over the world. Little do they know. My husband never takes a vacation. Every vacation turns out to be a business trip. The only time I see him is on the plane or ship. The minute we land some place, he gets in touch with some financial people and opens up a new branch. I am always alone.

"He is really in love with his business and not with me. I've known it for a long time. Once I told him how I felt and he replied, 'Would you be happier if I was a slob who didn't amount to anything?' Well, Ann, maybe I would. I'm miserable this way. No name, of course. Just sign this letter 'Money Isn't Everything.' "

Alcoholics, both men and women, are risky marriage gambles (in my book they are non-marriageables). When I receive a letter from a reader who is considering marriage to a heavy drinker, I do my best to knock it in the head. If the drinker will prove his willingness to submit to treatment, there may be a chance that the marriage will succeed. A young woman from Logansport, Indiana, wrote:

"He's a wonderful guy but liquor is his weakness. He tells me he drinks because he needs me so desperately. He promised to cut down as soon as we are married. What do you think, Ann?"

I told her (and all the others who have posed the question) that marriage has never been known to cure alcoholism. If the guy is serious about his desire to dry out, let him prove it *before* marriage by joining Alcoholics Anonymous or by availing himself of therapy. If he can stay out of the sauce for six months (and this means not a drop) then perhaps this marriage will succeed, but even then she should be aware of the risk involved.

Alcoholism is, of course, a symptom of other problems.

The man or woman who cannot handle his troubles and must seek solutions at the bottom of the bottle is better off unmarried. The grief alcoholics bring to their families is indescribable. In my view it is an act of charity for an alcoholic to stay single and not inflict himself on others.

Letters from homosexuals who despise the life they lead and yearn to be "like other people" give me a sense of helplessness because a cure for those who have reached the mid-twenties is extremely unlikely. Marriage does not qualify as therapy. I recommend psychiatric treatment because authorities agree that it can contribute to understanding and help them gain insight into their problem. The homosexual who believes he was "born wrong" (a theory which is generally unacceptable to psychiatrists) has a defeatist attitude and finds it difficult or impossible to adjust to conventional living.

In Dr. Albert Ellis' book, Sex Without Guilt, he says there is not an iota of clinical evidence that fixed homosexuality is inborn. He believes, rather, that it results from severe emotional damage in childhood. The homosexual who understands that his problem is an emotional one and not a physical defect and seeks therapy can sometimes make a good adjustment to single life.

Every non-marriageable type mentioned so far is an extreme neurotic. We have discussed the apron-string child who can't break away from mama or papa; the chronic chaser, both male and female; the unconscious coward who is afraid of marriage and doesn't know it (but manages to fall in a manhole just three steps shy of the altar); the undeveloped juvenile who is so in love with himself that he wants no part of sharing; the highly competitive woman who may need a bed partner but not a husband; the compulsive worker and the money grabber; the alcoholic and the homosexual.

Another non-marriageable type should be added to the list but it's difficult to label her because she doesn't fit into any of the categories mentioned so far. She appears to be perfectly normal. I use "she" because women dominate this group.

She is abnormal only in that she lacks the instinctive drive to marry or her drive is of such low voltage that she isn't even aware of it. I rarely receive letters from these women because they don't feel the need for advice. They are contented with their lot. For the most part they are school teachers, librarians, or secretaries—personable, well dressed, and well paid. They lead orderly lives and enjoy their work. They save money for that one big annual trip and then splurge. They enjoy their independence and wouldn't give it up unless someone "really wonderful" came along.

The sad truth is that their standards are unrealistically high. So they drift along, not unhappy, not depressed, not miserable, not filled with self-pity—a little lonely at times, but they have an orderly, uncomplicated life and this is what they really want.

Some non-marriageables are smart enough to know that marriage is not for them. Others learn too late. This letter is from a woman in Green Bay, Wisconsin:

> "I can't understand why the career girls who write to you feel they are missing so much in life by not being married. Where do they get the idea that a husband is the answer to everything? I wish one of those gals would take mine. I'm not bitter—just experienced.
>
> "Marriage is not the dream it's cracked up to be. I had a wonderful job when I married and gave it up to be a household drudge. I used to be a smart dresser but now I don't have the money to spend on clothes. When I was a career girl, my life was interesting. I met bright people,

I traveled, I spent my money as I pleased and didn't have
to answer to anyone.

"My husband is a nice guy, but he's dull. His idea of a
big evening is playing poker with the boys or falling asleep
in front of the TV set. I've had it both ways and let me
tell you that marriage is plenty over-rated. Many single
girls who write to you say they are lonesome. Well, I'm
married and I'm lonesome, too. To be perfectly honest,
I wish I were single again.

Ruth"

The next letter is from a career girl who echoes Ruth's
views. This woman, however, is unmarried and likes it. She
writes:

"When single girls write and ask you for advice on how
to snag a man, instead of outlining better trapping and
baiting methods why don't you tell them that for every
miserable old maid there are at least three unhappily married wives who wish they'd never seen the guy? Sure, some
of the girls who go through life unattached miss a few of
the grand privileges like squalling brats, interfering in-laws,
stingy husbands and the loss of freedom, but there are
many compensating rewards. The single woman who sup-
ports herself can travel, spend her money as she wishes,
have a date, a romance or a full-blown affair when she
feels like it. She can turn love off and on like an electric
bulb. So why don't you level with the girls, Ann?

Little Rock"

I agreed with Little Rock that marriage is not for everyone and that she is living proof. I explained that it takes a
special brand of tolerance to put up with squalling brats,
interfering in-laws and all the rest of her litany of grief.
Not everyone has it. I also told her that a woman who can
turn love off and on like an electric light bulb must have

a 25-watt heating system and that marriage demands more than that. I expressed the hope that she would not change her mind and marry some poor misguided man.

A life unmarried needn't mean a life wasted or a life of loneliness. Many unmarrieds enjoy full and purposeful years. They have time, energy and money to spend on community affairs and they are often valued and respected citizens.

Unmarrieds have their moments of self-pity, but then so do married people. For the singletons I leave this thought: Marriage is not for everyone. Your decision to go it alone may well have been best, considering your personality, instinctive drives and the goals you have set.

EIGHT

EIGHT

A life in your hands

P ARENTAGE," wrote George Bernard Shaw, "is a very important profession, but no test of fitness is ever imposed in the interests of the children."

And maybe it's a good thing. If the test of fitness were a written examination based on the theories advanced by many of our "experts," millions of successful parents would flunk. What we know about raising children is far less important than how we feel about children. Nature demands only that the biological requirements for parenthood be met. But parents have a moral obligation to provide their children with the emotional equipment to face life and measure up to its challenges.

Every parent wants to "do right" by his children. But what is "right"? Once upon a time (and not too long ago) mothers were told that a baby should be fed according to schedule. If he's asleep when it's time to eat, wake him up. If he gets up at dawn and howls for nourishment, let him cry until feeding time. Don't pick him up when he fusses or you'll spoil him. Teach him to walk as soon as he is able to stand. Start toilet training at six months. Parental instincts and baby's natural rhythm must be ignored. The clock was king.

Then along came new experts who decided the rigid approach was all wrong. The pendulum swung to the other extreme and the permissive school took over. Parents were instructed to throw away the clock. Feed the baby when he's hungry. Let him sleep when he feels like it. If he prefers to live it up at night and sleep during the day—get used to it. Never mind toilet training. Don't make an issue of it. He'll let you know when he's ready.

The permissive enthusiasts also set forth new rules for developing the "integrated personality." The central theme: permit the child to express himself. Don't inhibit him or you may damage his personality. If he wants to tear Aunt Ethel's feathered hat to pieces, let him. He may be acting out an urge to kill the canary.

When the products of permissive upbringing got into trouble in the school, the method began to be questioned. The young incorrigibles were labeled "anti-social" by their teachers. They "expressed themselves" by grabbing objects from other children and kicking the teachers. Since this was acceptable behavior at home, the child reasoned, it must be acceptable at school. The teachers wouldn't put up with it and the child had to learn new ground rules. The result, conflict and bewilderment.

Dr. Lee Kanner, a psychiatrist specializing in troubled children, wrote a book for laymen entitled *In Defense of Mothers*. In one passage Dr. Kanner said: "There is no air-raid shelter from verbal bombs that rain down on contemporary parents. At every turn they run up against weird words and phrases which are apt to confuse and scare them—words such as oedipus complex, maternal rejection, sibling rivalry, conditioned reflex, schizoid personality, regression, aggression, blah blah and more blah blah."

Dr. Kanner pleaded: "Mothers, let us together, regain the common sense which is yours."

The Menninger Foundation in Topeka, Kansas, conducted a revealing five-year study of infant development under the direction of Dr. Sibylle Escalona, a psychologist, and Dr. Mary Leitch, a psychiatrist. The project studied 128 infants from families of differing economic, social, educational and religious backgrounds. At home and at the hospital the babies were observed carefully day and night. A record was kept of each baby's reactions to sounds, objects, and people around him. Observations were made while the infants were feeding, playing and sleeping, when they were bathed and diapered.

The researchers were astonished at the wide range of behavior patterns among infants who were not yet one year old. Some babies were aggressive and daring, others were shy and withdrawn. Some were easily excited by outside stimuli, others were slow to respond to voices and the sight of food or toys. Some babies lost interest in a toy placed slightly beyond their reach while others howled and wriggled until the object was won.

Some babies got their best sleep during the day, others slept better at night. Some were sensitive to the faintest noises and awakened at the gentle sound of a flapping window shade; others slept blissfully while carpenters hammered new shingles on the roof of the nursery.

To the surprise of no intelligent mother the Topeka researchers concluded that hard and fast rules cannot be applied to all infants. Each baby has his own pattern of behavior. The wise mother tries to adapt to the needs of her own child.

The *method* of child raising, it was established, is far

less important than the *attitude of the mother*. The most valuable contribution a mother can make to the emotional development of her child is to love him. The well-informed woman who has read all the books (she may even be a specialist in child psychology) can fail as a mother if she lacks a genuine feeling of warmth for her child.

Loved people are loving people. The woman who was denied love and affection as a child is fortunate if she marries a man who can give her the assurance she lacked in childhood. The way a mother treats her child often reflects the love, or the lack of it, between husband and wife. Chances are a happily married wife will not resent the loss of sleep, the feeding demands or the interference with her freedom. And the husband who loves his wife takes pleasure in holding the child, feeding him and playing with him.

Warmth is caught, not taught. It is acquired through the heart, not the head. The sexually maladjusted, the impotent and the frigid who crowd our mental hospitals and divorce courts often trace their troubles to a deep-freeze early environment. One reader who complained about his wife's disdain for sex referred to her as "a chip off the old glacier."

Mother love is supposed to be instinctive. Our folklore tells us it is guaranteed to come packaged with every female, but not every woman has it. Few women are willing to admit, even to themselves, that they're incapable of mother love. But the tiniest infant can sense hostility and anxiety. Often a mother's milk does not "agree" with her baby because the mother is in a disturbed state. The mother who resents breast feeding her child may be able to fool her friends or herself but she can't fool the baby. The infant who has a serious feeding problem, skin rashes or other signs of disturbance should be under the supervision of a pediatrician, and the mother would be wise to seek professional help.

The healthiest, happiest babies are those who feel wanted and loved. The child born into a family of modest means, whose parents shower him with love and affection, has a better chance for sound emotional development than the child of wealthy parents whose major contribution is a sterile nursery and a high-priced governess.

One of the saddest letters I've ever received came from a father who wrote:

> "I am heartsick about our six-year-old son. For the third time he has been caught stealing at school. Twice he has taken small change out of the teacher's desk and yesterday he brought home a boy's ring which he said he found on the street. The teacher phoned to say she saw him take the ring off the wash basin.
>
> "I am at a loss to understand why Donnie does these things. We are able to buy the boy anything he wants. Why should he steal anything?
>
> "The moment the child was born he had every advantage. Although my wife and I travel a great deal, he is not neglected. We have an excellent staff of servants and he is never lonesome. This stealing has me worried sick. He won't talk about it; he just sits there looking sad. He treats me as if I were a stranger instead of his father who has given him everything. Please tell me what to do."

It is difficult to tell a father that he is making an emotional cripple of his son, but the evidence in this instance was irrefutable. Children who steal feel unloved. The child is saying "I can't have love so I'll take something else."

Toys and gifts do not take the place of parents who give time and attention to their children. I tell parents who write about similar situations to stop giving their children toys and money and start giving themselves!

A price tag on love

The child who misbehaves is frequently scolded and told that he is naughty or bad. This idea seems to be peculiar to our culture. When a French child misbehaves, his mother does not say "Be good!" She says "*Sois sage!*" which means "Be wise." The French child who behaves improperly is not "bad"; he is foolish. The Swedish mother admonishes her child with "*van snäll*" which means "be friendly." The Scandinavian culture views the undisciplined child as unfriendly or uncooperative. The German mother says "*sei artig*" which means "get in line." The German concept of good behavior is to conform.

Children should be taught that consideration for others is an essential part of good living. The child who satisfies his own comforts and desires at the expense of others should be told that he is unfair, not that he is bad.

If a child breaks the rules he must suffer the consequences but he should not be made to feel that he is unworthy of love. If it is meaningful, love is offered with no strings attached; it is unrelated to the behavior of the child.

All children disappoint us and fail us at times. This is an inevitable part of growing and learning. But children should not feel that they must earn love by being "good." Love is their natural inheritance. Children need unconditional love every day, regardless of what happened yesterday. To love a child when he is least lovable is the granite test of parenthood.

Favoritism and hostility

It is impossible for parents to have exactly the same feelings about all their children. It is natural to beam when a child wins honors. A youngster who is cooperative and lovable is bound to produce a warmer response than one who is sullen and troublesome. Perhaps the hardest test of parenthood is the capacity to pour out an extra measure of love and affection on the "difficult" child. And he is the one who most needs it.

If you were to ask parents which child in the family is the pet, most parents would deny there is a pet but if you were to ask the children, you'd probably get a specific answer. Often the pet wins his position by virtue of his sex. In a family of boys, a little girl is likely to be treated like a princess. Frequently, the first born is the favorite child because he gave his parents the first thrill of parenthood. Sometimes it's the baby of the family who gurgles his way into the special spot, because he's so tiny and cuddly— and perhaps unexpected. The child in the middle is rarely favored. He's edged out both ways and he can't win.

The cruelest tactic is to make a family pet of the child who happens to be the best looking. The son who is the image of his handsome dad is often favored over his brother who happens to look like a nondescript uncle from Keokuk. The girl who is a smaller version of her beautiful mother often moves in ahead of her plain sisters. And the extra attention the favorite gets from his parents is generously matched by the resentment of his brothers and sisters. Dr. Edward F. Litin, a psychiatrist at the Mayo Clinic, says it's no coincidence that the least attractive child in the family is so often the sickly one. When he finds he can't attract attention he develops asthma, headaches or he overeats. One of the angriest attacks from displeased readers was the consequence of this statement in my column:

> "It is not possible for a parent to love all his children 'the same.' No two children are 'the same.' A parent may love each of his children a great deal, but he loves them

in different ways and for different reasons. It is not infrequent for a parent to have a favorite."

This touched a raw nerve in hundreds of mothers. (Not a single father wrote!) The letters were both vitriolic and defensive. The guilt came through—loud and clear. I had the feeling that every mother who had a favorite child wrote to deny it.

I explained in a subsequent column (and hundreds of personal letters) that feelings cannot be weighed, measured, or put under a microscope. Furthermore, feelings change from day to day and sometimes from hour to hour. To say parents love all their children "the same" is an absurdity.

There is daily evidence in my mail to support my position. The problem, strangely, is often inverted. It is not about the favored child that many parents write but about the unfavored. This is logical since he is the problem. These lines from a Martin's Ferry, Ohio, mother describe the dilemma of the unfavored child:

> "I don't know what's wrong with Frank (not his real name, of course). He never seemed to fit into the family, even when he was a baby. My other children were all blonde and blue eyed. Frank was dark and puny and didn't even look like he belonged to us. He was in trouble from the minute he could walk. Now he's in jail for burglary and we aren't surprised. I always knew he'd end up bad."

It was an Eau Claire, Wisconsin, mother, however, who provided me with the classic example of the unfavored child who never had a chance. Although it's an extreme case, there is a lesson here for all parents. Many parents reject their children in subtle ways because of disappointment in the child's sex, looks, size, ability to learn, physical prowess, and on and on. The child senses this disappointment, quits trying to achieve anything and may even turn to being "bad" as an attention-getting device.

The Eau Claire mother wrote:

> "Our daughter Margaret is fourteen. This may be terrible for a mother to say but I wish that girl would walk out of the house and not come back. Margaret was a colicky, mean baby from the day we brought her home from the hospital. When she was three months old, she began to look just like my husband's sister Cora who was the town tramp. We noticed it when we had pictures taken.
>
> "Whenever I looked at Margaret I was reminded of Cora. By the time Margaret was three I was sure she had a bad strain in her. She broke every nice thing I had in the house and she kept running away. The more I spanked her the worse she got. Now she drinks and smokes and runs with a gang of hoodlums. We lie to protect her, but we know she's mixed up in something bad. Please tell me what to do before she gets her picture in the newspapers and disgraces us."

I advised the woman to contact the Family Service Association and request an appointment with a case-worker who could guide the disturbed girl. There was little value in pointing out that mother was 15 years late in seeking help for her daughter, and even later than that for herself.

Margaret Mead, the noted anthropologist, has pointed out that if we treat our children as we wish them to *be*, rather than as they are, they will try to live up to that lofty image. The Eau Claire mother wrote off her small daughter as a duplicate of Aunt Cora, the town tramp, and the girl proved that Margaret Mead's formula also works in reverse.

All parents (even "cold" ones) can give their children

some measure of strength and security by following a few basic rules. These rules can be applied in the rearing of all children from the day they are born.

Before formulating these guideposts for raising children I read stacks of books by acknowledged authorities in the field of child training. I also consulted experts who deal with problem children. And perhaps most important of all, I've had the benefit of a steady feed-back from thousands of letters written by parents who are living with these problems.

The books and authorities made one point abundantly clear. They said in effect "Everything we say may be wrong." I would like to say "amen" to that and re-emphasize that the instinct of a mother who loves her children is better than any authority. So—if none of these rules work for you, Mother, you can always take this book and whomp the kids with it.

1. Remember that a child is a gift from God, the richest of all blessings. Do not attempt to mold him in the image of yourself, your father, your brother, or your neighbor. Each child is an individual and should be permitted to be himself.

2. Don't crush a child's spirit when he fails. Never compare him with others who have done better. Dwell on what's right with him rather than what's wrong with him.

3. Remember that anger and hostility are natural emotions. Help your child find socially acceptable outlets for these normal feelings or they may be turned inward and erupt in the form of physical or mental illnesses.

4. Discipline your child with firmness and reason. Don't let your anger throw you off balance. If he knows you are fair you will not lose either his respect or his love. And make sure the punishment fits the crime because even the

youngest child has a keen sense of justice where he is directly concerned.

5. Parents should present a united front. Never join with your child against your mate. This can create emotional conflict within your child as well as in yourselves. It gives rise to destructive feelings of guilt, confusion, and insecurity.

6. Do not hand your child everything his heart desires. Permit him to know the thrill of earning and the joy of deserving. Grant him the satisfaction that comes with personal achievement.

7. Do not set yourself up as an example of perfection or of infallibility. This is a difficult role to play 24 hours a day, for years on end. You will find it easier to communicate with your child if you let him know that Mom and Dad can make mistakes, too.

8. Don't make threats when you are angry or wild promises when you are in an expansive mood. Threaten or promise only what you can live up to. To a child, a parent's word means everything. The child who has lost faith in his parent has difficulty believing in anyone or anything.

9. Do not smother your child with superficial manifestations of "love." The purest and healthiest love expresses itself in day-in-day-out upbringing which develops self-confidence and independence.

10. Teach your child that there is dignity in hard work, whether it is performed with calloused hands that shovel coal or skilled fingers that manipulate surgical instruments. Let him know that a useful life is a blessed one and a life of ease and pleasure-seeking is empty and meaningless.

11. Teach your child moral values. Personal integrity, truthfulness and the desire to treat others fairly are learned from your example. A child imitates the behavior of those

close to him. Parents whose daily lives reflect sound ethical standards provide their children with the basic tools for becoming decent human beings.

12. Do not try to protect your child against every small blow and disappointment. Adversity strengthens character and develops self-reliance. He can (and usually will) learn more from his failures than from his successes.

13. Don't always put your children first. Remember that parents are people, too. If you rush to satisfy his every whim, you will produce a self-centered juvenile, ill-equipped to fit into society. Parents who always place the wishes and comforts of their children first earn little gratitude—and no respect.

14. Remember the goal for all children should be independence. Don't cling to them or allow them to cling to you beyond the time when they should be on their own. The person who is always carried will never walk.

15. Teach your child to love God and to love his fellow man. Don't send your child to a place of worship—take him there. Children learn best from example. Telling him something is not teaching him. If you give your child a deep and abiding faith in God it can be his strength and his hope as well as his light when all else fails.

NINE

Father—or cash register?

A NOT-SO-FUNNY description of the American male goes like this: "A poor boob who is bossed by his mother, dominated by his wife, and hornswoggled by his daughter."

Historically, the role of the male has been that of provider, protector and undisputed head of the family. This picture of Family Life, U.S.A. has gone out of style. In by-gone days this phrase supported the old tintype, "I'll have to talk it over with my husband." Today, more frequently one hears, "I'll have to talk it over with my wife."

It has all happened in the past fifty years. And, curiously, the decline in status of the American male is not a result of anything he has done—or failed to do. The social evolution of the American female created "the great change." Women now have the vote. They hold public office, smoke on the street, drink in bars, wear slacks, and drive motorcycles. Women not only stand in buses, they drive them. Women practice law, medicine, dentistry.

They join the Army, Navy, Coast Guard, Marines and Air Force. Today, one out of three employed persons in the United States is a woman.

World War II gave the American woman her big boost in the man's world. When Rosie the Riveter donned overalls and pulled down $144 a week in take-home pay, it may not have dethroned dear old Dad but it surely made him move over. It was a financial advantage for the family but the cost was frequently expressed in the loss of domestic tranquility. The price in many families was dissension, delinquent children, and divorce.

Modern woman can do almost everything man can, except be a father. The rearing of emotionally healthy children requires the combined efforts of a Mom and a Dad. The divorcée or widow who carries the double load has a difficult time.

Too many fathers are floating unanchored—unsure of where they fit into the family picture. I concede that some dads don't *want* to fit into the family picture because it would interfere with their own selfish design for living. They don't want to be bothered. But other well-intentioned males have been shoved aside by domineering wives who would like to usurp the role of father as well as mother.

Despite the widely accepted assumption that the American male has been supplanted as head of the family, my readers tell me that a great many women not only *want* a husband to assume an active role, but that they *need* his help. The following letter from Minneapolis expresses a familiar complaint:

> "*Dear Ann Landers:* I am both mother and father to our four children. The youngest is two, the oldest is twelve. No, I'm not a widow. My husband is in excellent health, thank you. But he says the children are my job. He has never washed a face, changed a diaper, warmed a bottle, signed a report card, helped with a

homework lesson, played a game of ball or taken his sons anywhere. The only time he talks to his children is when he wants them to do something—and then it's an order, not a request. He never praises them, only criticizes.

"I know I can't change him. He's unbelievably obstinate. What I would like to know is how will the boys feel about their father when they grow up?

One Alone"

"Dear One Alone: When your children grow up they'll feel toward their father exactly as they feel now. They will hate him. The tiniest baby knows when he is loved and when he is being ignored. Children who are rejected by their father in infancy and scorned during adolescence because they don't do well enough to merit his praise suffer permanent emotional scars.

"When a parent writes and asks why his grown children are cold and indifferent, I tell him the chances are good that the kids had to wait until they grew up to get even."

Father Theodore Hesburgh, president of Notre Dame University, has said: "The most important thing a father can do for his children is love their mother." The husband who loves his wife shows it in subtle ways and their children sense it. An extravagant display of hugs and kisses or verbal mushing is no proof of love; it may well be a phony device to suggest love where there is none.

One of the best methods of showing love is by contributing one's physical presence—I mean by just being at home. A woman from Saginaw, Michigan, wrote a simple and heart-warming letter which expresses the thought eloquently:

"Many women write to you and complain because their husbands aren't very good company. They expect a man who has been working hard all day to come home at night and entertain them with interesting conversation. Usually what the man needs is a little peace and quiet and a chance to be himself. I learned this early in my marriage and it has saved a lot of wear and tear on my nerves.

"My George is not much to look at. He's a plain guy in many ways—no great reader or talker. I guess some women would consider him a dull clod. But just having him at home with me and the kids gives me a feeling of security. Some nights he doesn't say anything—just sits in the big chair and reads the paper and falls asleep in front of the TV. But when I can look across the room and see the big lug it gives me a feeling of peace and contentment. I wouldn't trade him for the world."

Many men make their living traveling and they must be away from their families for several days at a time. The mother should then do her best to be cheerful about his absence and explain that "Daddy is away because he must earn a living for us and this is the way he has to do it." When the traveling husband comes home, however, he should spend as much time as possible with his family.

Husbands who are absent three or four days almost every week and then devote Saturdays and Sundays to golf, fishing, or playing poker at the club abdicate their family responsibilities. They usually try to justify their behavior by saying they're entitled to a little relaxation because they pay the bills. These men are not fathers—they are cash registers. And when their children grow up, they will think of Dad's checkbook, rather than Dad.

Now, let's get specific. Just what is a father supposed to do? What is his function in the family, in addition to bringing home the bacon? Just being a man is probably the most important thing a father does. If children are to develop into well-adjusted adults they must know how men are supposed to act. Boys imitate their fathers and girls get notions of the kind of man they want to marry from observing their dads day after day.

When I was a youngster, I adored my father and I attributed to him all the wonderful qualities a man should have. I remember him as affectionate, big-hearted, impeccably groomed and he had a delicious sense of humor. He treated my mother as if she were a queen, but I never recall seeing my father in an apron nor do I ever remember seeing him perform a single domestic chore. Not that he was unwilling—my mother simply felt that the man of the household should be "above" kitchen tasks. This European approach, I am happy to say, died with that generation.

Particularly in families where both parents work, Dad should pitch in at home. There is nothing effeminate in a man drying dishes or running the vacuum sweeper. It takes a big man to do little things. It's healthy for children to grow up with the idea that a family is a cooperative organization and that everyone should work together in the common interest. If Mom takes a job downtown to help Dad, then Dad should help Mom at home if she needs a lift. And he should do it without complaint.

The cartoon stereotype that makes a sissy of the man who puts on an apron and helps at home is a fraud. And so is the notion that domestication is a sign of domination. The man who is sure of his masculinity isn't afraid of an apron.

In far too many families Dad has the role of the executioner who metes out punishment. This is unfair and it's also ineffective. The mother who threatens, "Wait 'till Daddy comes home—you're going to get it," does an injustice to both the child and the father. To a youngster, an hour can seem like a week. "When Daddy comes home" the child may well have forgotten the incident; and if he hasn't forgotten, the passing of time has made it seem unimportant.

I think it's obvious that no child should be slapped across the face or struck across the back, legs, or arms. Nature provided the ideal target. I am opposed to switches, straps, paddles, hairbrushes or other spanking paraphernalia. Again nature has provided the best implement—the human hand. The hand can strike as mighty a blow as any child should receive.

Dad represents the outside world. How he talks about his boss, the people he works with, his job, the government, the neighbors, minority groups—these are bits and pieces which sharply influence his children. Dad gives most children their basic ideas of what is right, what is fair, what is good, bad, and important.

There are exceptions, of course. They are the angry young men and women who fight whatever Dad is for—and champion whatever Dad is against. Familiar examples are the minister's son who winds up in jail or the industrialist's daughter who embraces extreme left-wing causes.

Most young children, however, accept the views expressed at home as gospel. If Dad says the Democrats are going to ruin the country with all their reckless spending, the kids believe it. If he says the Republicans are a pack of dinosaurs whose conservatism will finish us off, they believe it. If the American father knew how his children idolize him, he'd work harder to keep that hero image bright and shiny. To the child his Pop is the biggest and bravest and smartest man in all the world. Every child believes this —until he learns differently.

Daddy and his daughter

"Flowers on my shoulders
Slippers on my feet
I'm my daddy's darling
Don't you think I'm sweet?"

This jingle is familiar to every little girl who has ever taken elocution lessons. I suppose it has some charm when uttered by a four-year-old with a babyish lisp and it's particularly fetching with gestures, but when the little girl grows up, being "Daddy's darling" can mean trouble. Most little girls between the ages of two and seven think Daddy is the most wonderful man in the world.

A disturbed mother from Atlanta once wrote that she was terribly concerned about her only child—a six-year-old girl. She had overheard the youngster say to a playmate "When I grow up I'm going to marry Daddy. I don't know what we'll do with Mommy. We may have to send her on a long trip to China or something." I advised the mother that this was par for the course and it would be best to smile about it (to herself) and say nothing.

A father who is overly possessive can have a devastating influence on his daughter's reaction to men. Sometimes Dad unconsciously encourages dependency by saying in effect "You are Daddy's little girl and I'm not going to give you to anybody—ever." Such possessiveness can erect a difficult emotional hurdle for her as an adult. When a young man attempts to establish a romantic relationship she feels guilty and unfaithful to Daddy.

The father who knows how to express the proper kind of affection helps prepare her for mature womanhood. She grows up liking men and, equally important, she has the comfortable feeling that men like her. Such a girl has a healthy relationship with males and usually selects a loving husband—often someone who is surprisingly like Dad.

Some little girls are ignored, or worse yet, treated brutally by their fathers. Their personality patterns take on odd shapes and they become misfits in society. The girl who has been rejected or abused by her father sometimes becomes a man hater. If she does become involved with men, they are usually father substitutes toward whom she is punishing, hostile, sadistic or masochistic.

The girl who is ignored by her father feels unloved and unwanted. Promiscuous girls are usually searching for the love their fathers denied them. I have read numerous histories of delinquents and unwed mothers who were conditioned by such a home environment. In case after case the girl said, "My father never paid any attention to me. I wanted so much to have a man's arms around me that it didn't make any difference who he was."

Frequently I get letters from women who say they have difficulty writing because they can't see through their black eyes. The story is a familiar one—"John beat me up again—the fourth time this month." They go on to recite in detail histories of their bruises, loose bridgework and even hospitalization. The close of the letter is familiar too: "Please don't tell me to leave him. I love him very much and he's really a wonderful guy when he controls his temper."

And I don't tell them to leave. I advise them either to see a psychiatrist or to work out a rate with an ambulance service and a good dentist. It's clear that these women are mentally ill or they would not stick around for repeat performances. Their fathers beat them when they were growing up and they unconsciously picked out a man who reminded them of dear old dad.

Father and son

A great deal has been said and written about fathers being pals to their sons. I fell into a box of snakes when I printed the following letter and my reply:

> "My husband has been doing a good bit of reading on adult-child relationships and he has decided a father should be a pal to his son. Our only boy is ten. My hus-

band is forty-four. According to my husband most kids are scared stiff of their parents. He claims a relaxed 'buddy' atmosphere creates a healthy emotional climate. Some of our older friends who bought this theory raised spoiled, selfish kids who walk all over them. I don't go along with it personally, but he says it's sound. May we have your views?

Mommer"

"*Dear Mommer:* Your husband must be reading old books. Today it's the *parents* who are scared stiff of their children. Too much permissiveness has put youngsters in the driver's seat. A father should be a father. What ten-year-old kid wants a forty-four-year-old pal? A healthy father-son relationship is relaxed and friendly. When Dad too gets palsy-walsy, he destroys the symbol of authority which every child needs to guide him through childhood and adolescense."

An army of angry fathers swooped down to tell me I was all wet. The disagreement seemed to be based on semantics. I insisted there's a difference between "relaxed and friendly" and "palsy-walsy." They insisted that "pal" is a synonym for "friendly" and that I had goofed.

In one city at least, my timing couldn't have been worse. The day the column appeared in the New York *World-Telegram and Sun* under the heading "Ann Landers Says Dad Should Not Be A Pal To His Son," a nationally-known boy's organization launched its annual drive for better father-son relations. The slogan: "Be a Pal to Your Son."

Most sons idolize their fathers and look to them for leadership and strength. The father who tries to be a buddy destroys this image. A Dad need not be aloof or distant; the lines of communication should be kept open and accessible. A father should be able to have fun with his son—

even take some gentle ribbing—but he should be aware that he occupies a unique place in that boy's world. Underlying the fun and informality should be a feeling of respect. When I hear a young man tell his father to "Drop dead" . . . "Get lost" . . . "Pipe down" . . . the weaknesses of the pal system become all too apparent.

One of the saddest injustices that can befall a son is to be driven to excel by his well-intentioned father. Fathers on both ends of the success ladder are guilty. On the bottom rung is the man who never made the grade himself and longs to realize his shattered ambitions through his son. At the top of the ladder is the man who achieved great success and insists that his son be a carbon copy of the old man.

Both types are highly critical and often punitive. Frequently a boy will rebel against such pressures and withdraw from the competitive world. We all know unsuccessful sons of successful fathers and we wonder why the second generation didn't do better. Usually it's because their fathers drove them unmercifully and set standards which were impossible to meet. So the poor fellows, fearful of failure, gave up without even trying.

The most challenging aspect of being a father—and a mother, too—is knowing when to remove the safety net and let your children learn their own lessons.

Parents can do many wonderful things for their children, but they cannot drill holes in their heads and pipe their knowledge and experience into them. Nor should parents want to, for learning is a glorious experience. And young people can never achieve self-respect and independence unless they can learn to take their own lumps.

However, parents can give their children love, understanding, strength and a good example to follow. Children who inherit these gifts are the richest of all. And such a legacy never leaves the family. It appreciates in value as it is handed down from generation to generation.

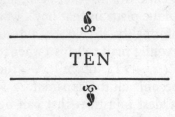

TEN

The war between the siblings

"The wrath of brothers is fierce and devilish . . ."
Thomas Fuller, 1732

"*Dear Ann Landers:* I am a girl eleven years old who is very sad. My father carries a picture in his wallet of my sister who is sixteen. She is very pretty. I am ugly compared to her. Everyone tells her how beautiful she is and she sure does know it by this time.

"My father also carries a picture of my little brother who is seven. He looks just like Daddy which makes him the second favorite in the family. My father doesn't carry my picture at all. I gave him my picture and made sure it would fit in his wallet. It wasn't very pretty but it looks like me. He put it in the drawer. What can I do to get him to carry my picture?

Left Out"

I told "Left Out" her Daddy probably had forgotten where he had put the picture. I suggested that she remind him—and show him this column.

Jealousy between brothers and sisters has existed since Cain slew Abel. The Bible, Greek mythology, ancient and current history are rich with examples of hatred and bitterness among brothers and sisters. There's a clinical term for it—"sibling rivalry." The word sibling means children of the same parents. It comes from the Anglo-Saxon word *sibb*, meaning relatives.

"Man's inhumanity to man makes countless thousands mourn—" and when the man (or woman) is a member of the same family, the wounds are deeper and the suffering is more acute. Jealousy, aggression, dependency, the desire to dominate, and an assortment of other unhealthy emotions are easy to recognize in younger children, but they exist in adults too—sometimes in an intensified form. Childhood hostilities are frequently never resolved—they merely go underground.

Adults have more complicated sibling troubles because they involve in-law problems—not only father- and mother-in-law but sister- and brother-in-law. It's a husband who writes to complain that his wife is so attached to her brother that she neglects the marriage. Or it's a wife who writes that her husband's sister (or brother) dominates him and he's afraid to open his mouth.

Brothers and sisters who grow into adulthood, bossing and making demands on one another, frequently are unable to break these childhood patterns. The result can be a shattered marriage. Here are two examples:

> "My wife's brother lives with us and she waits on him hand and foot. He hasn't worked in four months. When I tell her he's got to find a job or get out, we have a big fight and she starts to cry . . ."

"My husband is in business with his brothers. He works harder than all of them put together, but we don't have a thing to show for it. They all live swell but we have to struggle to get by. I've begged him to talk about more money but he always finds some excuse. There ought to be a law against brothers being in business together."

Adults who are unable to break away from their brothers and sisters are emotionally immature. There are countless combinations of such neurotic entanglements and the story of how they got that way can usually be traced to Mom and Dad.

Parents who treat each child fairly help them to build the foundation for a stable relationship in later years. The favorite child or the "family pet" is heir to the hostility of his brothers and sisters. If there are special favors or privileges to be had, the children should share them or have them in turns. The child who always gets the breaks because he is the oldest or the youngest or the prettiest or the smartest pays a dear price for this preferred treatment.

School teachers sometimes create bitterness among brothers and sisters by thoughtlessly making comparisons. It is natural for Miss Jones to identify Willard Smith with his brother Oscar. But it can be catastrophic if Oscar is brilliant and industrious and Willard is mediocre and somewhat lethargic. The teacher who makes the mistake of saying "I can't understand why you don't do better—your brother was such a fine student!" does more damage than she knows—and she injures the relationship, too, because the one who suffers by comparison cannot help but dislike the brother who has put him in an unfavorable light.

Many an adult is driven by destructive feelings of competitiveness with brothers or sisters. The childhood wounds still hurt. To the one who was always "second best," it doesn't matter that he is now grown and eminently successful. He must still convince the brothers or sisters that he is successful. How do these feelings start? No one knows exactly why, but there is one axiom: Every child wants to be the favored one, whether he is the first born or the seventh born. Each child wants all the love, all the attention and all the toys. As an only infant he gets all of everything. When he is obliged to share, he surrenders every priority with reluctance. He battles against dethronement.

Sibling rivalry can be a manageable family problem or it can be an endless round of tattling, fighting, head-bashing, and refereeing. It all depends on how parents handle it. If the problem is dealt with realistically and intelligently, brothers and sisters have a minimum of squabbles (preferably settled among themselves) and they grow up with mutual respect and admiration. If the problem is not handled intelligently, brothers and sisters can turn a home into a battleground, drag parents into the struggle, demand that parents make choices. The result: wild competitiveness and lifelong hostilities.

Parents with more than one child must accept the fact that there is rivalry among *all* children. Because rivalry often has an unattractive face, many parents pretend it doesn't exist. In an effort to present a family portrait of bliss and perfect harmony (artificial, of course, because no family achieves this) they say: "Our children adore each other. There is no competitiveness in our family. It's all for one and one for all."

If parents really believe this rubbish, they've been hoodwinked by their kids. Children are infinitely clever at concealing their real feelings. In most families there is some open warfare among brothers and sisters. Conflict is inevitable and should be tolerated, within limits. Honest expression of anger is far healthier than smiling on the outside and boiling on the inside. But parents must never allow themselves to be drawn into the petty squabbles of their children—comforting the one who complains first or who cries the loudest. When such false rewards can be won, the fighting is endless.

The art of buck-passing is an All-American family sport which is readily learned when parents fail to act with authority. Every child should be taught early that a request from parents is a politely worded order—not a trial balloon sent up to see what will happen.

Every child should be assigned small chores which benefit the entire family—emptying the trash baskets, going to the grocery store, or bringing in the wash when it rains. They should accept the proposition that it is honorable to be a contributing member of a group and dishonorable to be a loafer or a goldbrick.

When there are no assigned duties it's easy to pass the buck or evade the responsibility entirely. Children who are not made to feel responsible for chores consider "work" and "errands" dirty words. The brothers and sisters then compete for the title of "most idle."

The scene that follows is enacted in thousands of homes daily. If it sounds like a tape-recording made in your home, you have work to do.

Mother: "Mary, please go to the grocery store and get a loaf of bread and two quarts of milk. We need them for supper."

Mary: "Gee, Mom, I went to the store yesterday. Make Jimmy go."

Jimmy (who enters the room at that moment): "No fair. I went to the drug store for Pop's pipe tobacco last night. Besides, I'm just leaving—promised to play first base. So long."

Mother: "Jimmy said he went to the drug store for Dad last night, so you'll have to go, Mary."

Mary: "That rat! I heard him tell Dad he *wanted* to go to the drug store for airplane glue and Dad said as long as he was there to get him some tobacco."

Mother: "Oh, is that the way it was? Well, anyway he *did* go, and I need the things so please be a good girl and do this for Mother."

Mary: "Gee, Mom, I'm right in the middle of an English paper. I have to finish it by tomorrow. You don't want me to flunk, do you? Bobby will be home from school in a few minutes. Ask him."

Scene Two: Mother (weary of the buck-passing and excuses) puts on her sweater and heads for the grocery store.

Another effective device designed to trap parents into displaying favoritism is the old-fashioned tattle-tale game. Billy comes rushing into the kitchen, sobbing and screaming. His words are barely understandable.

"Louise threw dirt in my eyes—and I didn't do anything to her," he sobs.

Louise appears in the doorway and shouts "That's a lie. Billy threw dirt on me first. He was hiding behind the garage and he thought I didn't see him."

Billy: "I did not!"

Louise: "You did, too. . . ."

Mother: "Louise, shame on you for treating your little brother like that. Just for that, no movie for you Saturday."

The moment Mother turns her back Billy is all smiles, sticks out his tongue at his older sister and says "Ha, ha, I sure got you in Dutch."

There is no perfect solution but the best way to discourage such performances is to penalize both parties. It's a waste of time, patience and energy to try to determine who started a fight between two kids. The one who gets his story told first usually wins.

It should be understood that the peace and quiet of the home is not to be disturbed by indoor fighting and tale-bearing. Teach your children to settle their differences out-side—between themselves. When they discover that run-ning to Mom or Dad with reports will bring punishment to both parties, the back-biting stops. The idea behind tattling is to win favored treatment, or at least to put the other one in bad. When children find it won't work, they learn to live together. After all, what's the fun in fighting when no one is around to listen and nothing can be gained?

Many parents invite hostility between children by per-mitting the younger one to tag along with the older one and enjoy the same privileges even though there may be an age spread of as much as four or five years. If the older child resents this and complains, he is told that he must not be selfish and that he must be good to his younger brother or sister.

The older child feels abused and his hostility for the younger one grows by the minute. He is sure the parents love the younger one more and as proof points to the fact that "Bob gets cut in on everything that is mine."

This is a double-edged sword. The younger child be-comes overly aggressive toward the older one because he feels he is immune to punishment. Dick has heard Mom and Dad tell Victor that he is responsible for "his younger brother" and therefore Dick does as he pleases. If something goes wrong, Victor gets the blame because he is older.

Older children should not be saddled outside the home with younger brothers or sisters. They should give Mom a hand if help is needed, but they should not be asked to share their friends, clothing, possessions, or interests.

Many unhappy teen-agers write to complain that the oldest child is the pet of either Mom or Dad or both. In many families the first-born gets the inside track, but this does not mean he should reign as Queen or King of the household, ordering the younger ones around as if they were lackeys. Older children should not be permitted to push their chores on to the younger ones. Nor should they be permitted to help themselves to the possessions of the younger ones just because they are older.

Hand-me-downs

In families where there are several children, regardless of the available financial resources, it is not uncommon for the younger ones to wear "hand-me-downs." The psychological effect can be devastating if it is not done with love and understanding. The following lines from a young girl in Charleston, West Virginia, poignantly illustrates the heartache:

> "I'm thirteen years old and I have never had a dress that was bought just for me. I have two older sisters and every dress I ever had was a hand-me-down. Some of them are in pretty good condition if my sisters get tired of them in a hurry. I can't wait until I am old enough to quit school so I can go to work and buy some brand new clothes that have never been worn by anyone else."

I make it a rule never to volunteer unsolicited advice, but I had a difficult time restraining myself in this case. I wanted desperately to write to this girl's mother and plead with her to buy the child the next new dress in the family. I ached to tell her, no matter how much the older ones may *think* they need a new dress, it is not nearly so important as getting this thirteen-year-old a dress just for her.

Boys usually pay less attention to clothes but the younger male animal can also have feelings of being second and third best if he is forever handed down the used clothing of an older brother. Every child should have something new which was purchased (or made) just for him—at least once in a while.

How parents help brothers and sisters hate each other

Several years ago in Chicago, an eighteen-year-old boy murdered a stranger who was sitting on a park bench. "Why did you do it?" he was asked by the police. "Because my mother kept telling me I should be like my older brother. My brother was always winning honors and things. I could never be like him, so I decided to be just the opposite. This was the worst thing I could think of to do."

It's too bad an automatic gag can't be applied to parents just before they utter these poisonous words: "Why don't you behave more like your older brother or sister?" If there is a more inflammatory sentence in the English language, I don't know it.

It is marvelously healthy for younger brothers and sisters to want to imitate the good behavior of their older siblings, but they must do so because of honest admiration. An order to "behave like Brother Jack" usually insures contrary behavior. There is enough natural competitiveness between siblings without encouraging more.

When Alice comes home with a beautiful report card, studded with A's and glowing compliments on her conduct, it is natural (and correct) for the parents to show pleasure and to praise her. On the other hand, her brother Phil, who is two years younger, brings home a card which indicates he may flunk English and spelling and that his math is borderline. In addition to poor marks, his deportment suggests that he is unwilling to accept direction and that he is not working up to his capacity.

It would be preposterous for parents to congratulate Phil on such a card, but he should be dealt with privately—and independently of his sister. No comparisons should be made between his card and Alice's. Phil knows he has done poorly and that his sister has done well. When his parents set his sister up as the model, he feels justified in hating her. In his confusion and anxiety, she becomes the source of his troubles. He figures if it weren't for her he wouldn't look so bad. His major concern then is not how to do better but how to get even with his sister.

Love each other—or else!

Too many parents force togetherness on their children in the hope that it will make them devoted. Children have more in common with youngsters their own age than with siblings who are a few years older or younger.

It would be a better world and a safer world if all people, everywhere, loved and respected each other—but they don't; and so long as the human animal remains basically unchanged, they never will. But we should be able to learn to live together harmoniously. This cannot be accomplished in a family by demanding or begging children to love each other—"or else." It can be achieved only by raising children to be independent, self-sufficient, and genuinely considerate of one another. The healthiest sibling relationships are those which flower naturally out of trust, respect, and admiration.

But brothers and sisters are held together by a mysterious bond for as long as they live. The experiences shared while growing up give their relationship a unique dimension.

Brothers and sisters must *like* each other before they can love each other. And they will like each other only if they feel they have been treated honestly and fairly. It is the parents who set the emotional thermostat in the home. If parents are fair to each child and if they encourage each one to have his own interests, the children, when they grow to adulthood, will not feel the need to compete with each other financially, socially, or professionally. They will not feel the compulsion to "keep up with" or to overwhelm each other. They will have quiet feelings of pride in the achievements of one another. They will seek each other out as friends because they thoroughly enjoy being together. And this is the highest compliment of all.

ELEVEN

Double trouble

T HIS SHOULD NOT be a chapter. It should be a volume.
Years before I dreamed of becoming an advice columnist, I promised myself I would one day write a book on
rearing twins. I know how it looks from the inside, because
my twin sister and I were practically Siamese from the day
we were born to the day we married—and naturally it was a
double wedding.

I have attempted to read everything available on the subject of twins. I have observed twins, questioned their parents, their brothers and sisters, their friends and their
teachers. And now, as Ann Landers, I receive a great many
letters from twins. It is disturbing to me that in the past
twenty years I have encountered so few twins whose parents
are doing an enlightened job of raising them. I do not say
this in criticism. If the parents *knew* better, they would *do*
better. But unfortunately, there has been precious little information available to help parents raise twins.

The most common and most damaging error is to assume that because twins came into the world together they must be dressed alike, encouraged to do the same things, and instructed to stick together, come what may. This is precisely what should *not* be done.

It is of course easier to treat twins as a single unit rather than as two individuals. It requires extra time and energy and imagination to steer children of the same age in separate directions. It is infinitely simpler for the parents if twins go everywhere together, share each other's friends, clothes, and interests. And then, too, twins boost the parental ego. It makes them feel "special" (for dad, a better word is virile) because a multiple birth falsely suggests extraordinary sexual prowess. So how do you let the world know? By dressing your twins alike, parading them as a unit, and keeping them together. This may do wonders for mama and papa, but it triggers serious problems for the twins.

It may be rewarding to review the application of conflicting theories in the rearing of two sets of quintuplets. One set was kept together; the other was split up.

On May 28, 1934, near Callander, Ontario, five little girls were born to Oliva and Elzire Dionne. Dr. Allan Roy Dafoe, a country doctor, delivered the quintuplets at home and is credited with having saved their lives. The Dionnes were the first quints in medical history to survive more than a few hours. Lillian Barker, a newspaper woman and friend of the Dionne family, told the inside story of the celebrated quints in her book "The Dionne Legend."

Author Barker described how Dr. Dafoe became a jealous foster parent. He threatened to walk off the case if anyone questioned his handling of the children and "ran the whole show to suit himself."

Time Magazine (March 26, 1951) said: "Dr. Dafoe engineered the deal which took the quints from their parents and made them the wards of the Ontario government. He moved them into a private nursery and granted the parents permission to visit—provided they showed their passes."

Dr. Dafoe signed movie contracts, made broadcasts, endorsed medicine, baby products, and cereals. Souvenir stores sprang up in Callander and the quints became an international attraction. Visitors (armed with an admission ticket) were permitted to look in on the quints through a one-way glass window. In 1935 Papa and Mama Dionne went on a stage tour.

Dr. Dafoe died in 1943, but his policies were pursued. The quints were to be raised together, dressed alike, separated from their parents and other brothers and sisters and publicized as a single unit. Then, a year after Dr. Dafoe's death, Mr. and Mrs. Dionne succeeded, through an act of Parliament, in getting their children back. The quints were ten years old when they moved out of the display quarters into the family home. By then their personality patterns were set. They were shy and clung together. They didn't want to be out of one another's sight. When they were graduated from high school at the age of eighteen, none had ever been out on a date alone with a boy.

In 1943, on July 15, another set of quintuplets was born in Buenos Aires, Argentina. Three girls and two boys, each weighing two pounds, were born to Maria and Franco Diligenti.

But the world did not know about the Diligenti quintuplets until they were almost eight months old. Their multimillionaire father had been advised by a physician and close friend to shun all publicity and to rear the children as individuals.

The children were registered in widely-separate localities so that their multiple birth would be kept a secret. It leaked out several months later, but Papa Diligenti still managed to keep them shielded from publicity and exploitation. He had the means to stick to his program.

Each quint had a separate room and a private nurse from infancy. At the age of seven they were sent to separate schools, miles apart. They were permitted to be together only during vacations.

At the age of nine and a half, the Diligenti quintuplets received their first public attention on the occasion of their first Communion. The world had its first look at the quints, and it found them healthy, energetic, outgoing and filled with the excitement of living. Each quint was lavishly endowed with self confidence and a distinct personality. They spoke four languages—Spanish to each other, Italian to their parents, English at school, and French when needed.

Following the Communion Mass, there was a garden party for 400 adults and school mates on the Diligenti estate. The quintuplets were friendly to each other, but they did not huddle together. They went off in separate directions and played with their school mates.

The chances of having quintuplets are 1 in 57 million, so therefore it's unlikely that anyone reading this book will be faced with the problem. The chances of having twins, however, are about 1 in 87. If it happens to you, the most important thing to keep in mind is this: treat twins as separate and distinct personalities. Remember that each is a person. Each has an ego. Rear them as individuals and not as a single unit.

My number one rule for rearing twins: do not dress them alike

This is so important that I'm asking the printers to put it in great big type. I repeat—DO NOT DRESS THEM ALIKE!!

Dressing twins alike is exploitative and it is destructive.

Why? Because it is an attention-getting device to accentuate their similarities. This defeats the prime objective, which is to encourage the development of separate personalities.

Whenever I see a pair of carbon copies on the street with their mother, I am seized by an almost uncontrollable desire to stop the woman and say "For heaven's sake, please stop dressing those children alike!" (I have done this on occasion and have been rewarded for my free, unsolicited advice with a "you must be nutty" look.)

When I have suggested in my column that twins not be dressed alike, irate mothers let me know in no uncertain terms that their twins *want* to dress alike. Of course they do. But the mothers should not permit it.

A mother in Madison, Wisconsin, wrote to say her twin daughters made a great effort to look as much alike as possible. One had a natural mole on her left cheek. The other twin penciled in a matching mole with a crayon. "They spend hours pinning up their hair exactly alike," the mother wrote. "I don't think this is good. Why do they do it?"

I gave the mother this answer:

> "Your twins are using their twinhood as a gimmick to attract attention. It works. It sets them apart from the crowd at once. Identical twins are on stage at all times. The average singleton hasn't a chance in a room with a pair of identically-dressed twins. Don't let your twins use an accident of nature to put themselves over. Encourage them to develop individual personalities. They may resist your efforts at first, but in the long run they will be much happier because you laid down the law."

My number two rule: separate your twins in school if it is possible

Twins in a classroom (a) get more than their share of attention (b) confuse the teacher (c) lean on one another for support (d) work less effectively than if they were strictly on their own.

In rural areas, separate schools present a formidable problem. The rural family that can afford to send twins to separate private schools is fortunate. If the family lives in a city where there are several public schools, the problem of transportation for one twin is a nuisance, but the rewards justify the effort.

My twin sister and I were in our second year at North Junior High School in Sioux City, Iowa, when two enlightened teachers, Miss Olive Jones and Miss Irma James, decided that we (the Friedman twins) should be split up. No teacher had thought of it before. When we received our home-room assignments and discovered we were to report to different rooms, we kicked up such a fuss that one would have thought the school officials had plotted to send one twin to Siberia and the other twin to Hong Kong.

Hand in hand we marched to the principal's office. We presented a picture of solidarity that would have made Damon and Pythias look like strangers. "You can't separate us," we moaned. "We'll just die!"

The principal was a gentle soul. He listened patiently as we stated our case. He made a major concession. We could be together for two subjects, but we must remain in separate home-rooms. This was a partial victory but we were less than jubilant. However, during the first week of separation, my twin was elected president of her home-room. This was the first time either of us had been given individual recognition, and I'm sure it was one of the happiest days of her life.

Through the remaining years in junior high school we were separated part-time, and we did not object. I think we even secretly enjoyed it, but to have admitted as much openly would have been traitorous.

When we entered Central High School, we had the privilege of selecting subjects and teachers, and I am sorry to say we slipped back to the sure-fire, attention-getting tricks. We selected every course together, once more casting ourselves in the roles of Kate and Dupli-Kate. For the next three years we were side by side in every class—confusing the teachers, overwhelming the boys, antagonizing the girls, and playing the double exposure for all it was worth.

My number three rule: encourage twins to follow separate interests and develop their individual talents

Because two people may look alike to the casual observer does not mean that they think alike or that they have identical personalities, work-habits, or talents.

My twin sister and I both studied the violin. Half of our dear father's money was wasted. The half spent on lessons for me went down the drain. I had little interest in the violin, but it takes two to make a duet and I guess we did look pretty cute playing our violins together. It was small wonder my sister played the violin better than I. In addition to having a natural talent for the instrument, which I lacked, she took a good many more lessons. My twin frequently substituted for me because I didn't like to practice.

I realize now that I lacked the initiative in my teen years to develop my own special talents—writing and public speaking. Instead of fiddling around with the fiddle and being part of a duet, I should have been on the debating team, working on the year book, or writing editorials for the school paper. It is unfortunate that some older and wiser head did not recognize this. With the proper guidance I might have found my place many years earlier. I loved to write, I loved to talk, and I loved to crusade for causes. But it wasn't until many years later that I was able to break up the vaudeville act and function as a whole person.

My number four rule: separate fields of endeavor will avoid head-on-clashes or—worse yet—below the surface hostilities

In my opinion, twins should not compete in the same field. Such competition may produce a champion, but it is far more important to produce two healthy personalities.

The following letter from a mother of twin sons was interesting because she wrote for help with a problem which was actually only a symptom of the main trouble.

She wrote:

> "*Dear Ann Landers:* My twin sons are seventeen years old and if I say so myself, they are handsome. I am worried about them because they have no interest in girls, although the girls seem to be crazy about *them.* They get frequent telephone calls from girls, but I have to push them to go to parties and take dates.
>
> "It seems my twins have only one interest in life—golf. They are on the golf course almost every day after school until it is too dark to see the ball. Weekends are always spent playing golf. Both boys are excellent golfers, but one twin has won more tournaments and cups than the other. They usually practice together, although sometimes they will play in a foursome. They have no interest in playing in separate foursomes."

The mother added a telling P.S.:

> "My twins are devoted to each other. There is no rivalry between them. They haven't had a fight in years.

I think it's marvelous that they love each other so dearly, but I do wish they would get interested in girls before they go to college in the fall. Can you suggest something?

Mother"

Mother was, of course, off in Disneyland. She had no understanding of what was going on in the minds and hearts of her sons. She did not realize that her twins who "have not had a fight in years and love each other dearly" were fighting it out daily on the golf course. They had no interest in girls because their energies were directed into another channel. These boys were each consumed with a single interest—to beat out the other one. This was more fun than girls.

I advised the mother to send the boys to different colleges. I went further. I told her, if necessary, to *forbid* them to go to the same school. I explained that they were too tied up with one another, and too competitive. Separated, I suggested, their interests would fan out in a variety of healthy directions—including girls.

Mother shot back a reply informing me that I was "out of my mind." She said I had a lot of nerve suggesting that her sons were trying to out-do each other. Furthermore, my recommendation that they be sent to different colleges was downright cruel. She wrote, "God meant them to be together. He sent them to us together. It would be a sin to separate them."

I replied:

"God did not join these two at the hip. He gave them separate bodies, separate minds and separate nervous systems. God sent you *two* human beings. He meant them to be individual personalities. I hope you will cooperate with Him and help each of your sons to lead his own life."

Mother never wrote again—and it was just as well. She was beyond my reach. It was like trying to bore through a concrete wall with a toothpick.

My number five rule: do not compare one twin with the other and do not permit friends and relatives to do it

I grew up with a pair of deep dimples. My twin sister had no dimples. Thoughtless people often said to her, "How does it happen that your twin has dimples and you don't have any?" I can't say for certain how my twin felt on hearing this inane question hundreds of times—but I can imagine.

No mention should be made of differences between twins. If one twin boy is smaller than his brother, you can bet he is sensitive about it. On one occasion I heard an adult ask a nine-year-old who was noticeably smaller than his twin brother, "Why don't you grow faster and catch up with your twin brother?" The child was crestfallen and stood silent. My blood pressure had risen about 20 points, and I turned to the adult and said, "What's so special about being bigger than somebody? I always went for the short fellows myself. What counts is not being short on brains."

The nine-year-old looked at me with the most grateful eyes I'd ever seen. "Gee," he beamed, "I'll have to remember *that* one!"

On another occasion when I spoke in San Bernardino, California, several young people crowded around after the speech. A pair of identically-dressed twin girls asked for my autograph. One of the girls said with an air of false bravado, "We're twins—but my sister is prettier." My heart went out to her because I knew that she had heard this from others many times—and she had learned to protect herself against the hurt by saying it first.

I told the little twin that I would give her my autograph in exchange for hers—and to write down her address because I wanted to drop her a note. She was delighted. The following week I sent her a four page typewritten letter on "twinship" and told her never again to mention her sister's better looks or to feel that it made *her* second best. I told her that looks don't matter to people who are worth knowing. It's how we live, how we treat others, and what we can contribute that counts.

She replied:

> "*Dear Ann Landers:* I will keep your letter forever. You will never know what you have done for me."

Parents can protect their twins against thoughtless comparisons by stopping people dead in their tracks with "We never compare our children—if you don't mind."

My number six rule: encourage your twins to be honest and open about their feelings

There is competition between all brothers and sisters. This is natural and it is normal. Twins can be twice as competitive—and they usually are. Parents who fail to understand this make real trouble for their twins. Twins should not be made to feel guilty or disloyal if they don't stick together on all things.

I remember the sense of guilt I suffered when, at the age of eleven, I screwed up the courage to express a preference for shredded wheat over puffed rice. I had been brought up to feel that "everything with twins should be alike." I knew my sister preferred puffed rice and she knew I preferred shredded wheat—so we used to alternate. One day both of us would eat puffed rice, and the next day we'd both have shredded wheat. It was a momentous morning when I announced, "Look, you can eat puffed rice every day if you want it, but I'm having shredded wheat." She was perfectly agreeable, but I'm sure she felt as I did that somehow we were letting our mother down.

Twenty-three years later, in 1952, I supported Adlai Stevenson for President. My sister supported General Eisenhower. We reminded each other of the shredded wheat and the puffed rice and laughed about it. In spite of the passing of many years, however, there were still twinges of guilt because we were not "sticking together." It was nobody's fault. The early training had left its mark—and the roots were deep.

Parents of twins should encourage their children to be individuals, to feel free to disagree. Twins should develop their own likes and dislikes. They should cultivate their own friends, hobbies and interests. Every twin should paste this motto where he can look at it every day: *"The one thing that I can do better than anyone else is to be myself."*

TWELVE

How well do you know your teen-ager?

"Children need models more than they need critics."
Joseph Joubert, 1842

WHEN I WAS YOUR AGE . . ." What parent has never uttered this poisonous phrase? What teen-ager doesn't regard it as the prelude to the dreariest of all monologues?

Our children don't want to hear about how we did things when we were their age. In the first place, it's difficult for them to believe we ever were. And somehow we always manage to sound as if we were better behaved, harder working, more sensible and more respectful. Do you enjoy listening to little stories in which the narrator is the hero—and, by implication, you are the villain? Neither do your children.

What were you really like when you were a teen-ager? It's not easy to remember, particularly the unpleasant things. We bury a great deal of what we don't want to remember by blocking out the painful experiences. After a while it's almost as if they never happened. And this is good because if we had to begin each day with a vivid memory of yesterday's wounds, the suffering would be intolerable.

But just for now, try to think back to your teen years. How did you feel about yourself—and others? Did you make friends easily or did you feel a little "out of it"? Were you relaxed about your friendships or were you competitive with others for the attention of the people you liked best? Were you always as sure of yourself as you wanted the world to believe? Or was part of your outer confidence bluster and bluff? Were you your best self at all times or did you trim a little here and cheat a little there?

How did you feel about your parents? Did you ever feel that they were too old-fashioned, too demanding, too narrow minded or perhaps downright stupid? Did you ever feel unwanted, unloved, and completely worthless?

What was your atttiude toward sex? Did your mother or father ever talk to you about it? If you are in your forties or older, chances are that the subject was taboo in your home. So you grew up with the vague feeling that there was something terribly wrong with it. Sex thoughts made you feel guilty and ashamed.

Where did you get your sex information? Probably from friends. In every teen-age circle there was someone who knew more than the rest. They learned it from the maid, or the yardman, or they eavesdropped on older brothers and sisters. One thing was certain—you knew a lot more about sex than your parents thought you did. And your children know more about sex than you think they do, too.

When I was eleven years old, I sent away for a leaflet

called "Margaret Mae's Twelfth Birthday." When it arrived (in a plain envelope) I slipped down to the basement storage room with the leaflet tucked in the sleeve of my sweater. I recall my eager anticipation. After reading two pages I was sure I'd been swindled. I felt like writing and asking them to return my dime. There wasn't a bit of information in that leaflet that I hadn't known for at least three years. I could have written a better one myself!

In the teen-age circles of yesteryear someone in the crowd usually managed to get his hands on a little booklet called "The Art of Making Love." It had diagrams and some big words which nobody understood—but you got the idea. The booklet was passed around until it was dog-eared and nearly illegible. It was exciting to read such things, but all the while you had the nagging suspicion that you were evil and that sex was unclean and nasty.

The booklet raised many questions in your mind. There was a lot about it that you didn't understand. You were eager to learn the answers, but you couldn't go to your parents because they might be shocked. Besides, you never thought of your parents as people who would know anything about sex. They seemed so proper.

If we can recapture our own teen-age experiences, we will be better able to understand our children. Armed with understanding we can guide them along the path of maturity and useful living.

Have you ever wondered what your teen-agers think of you? Well, I can tell you that their ideas change from day to day and from week to week. A boy of thirteen will have a vastly different view of his father by the time he has reached his eighteenth birthday. An old joke illustrates the teen-ager's shifting appraisal of his father—the joke about the eighteen-year-old boy who announced, "When I was thirteen my Pop didn't know a darned thing. He was the dumbest cluck who ever lived. It's amazing how much the old man has learned in the last five years."

The most difficult years for teen-agers are from fourteen to seventeen, depending on the rate of their glandular and emotional development. The transition from adolescence to young adulthood can be a frightening experience. This is the age of self-consciousness, of long arms and big feet. Teen-agers need an extra dose of love and moral support during these awkward years when they seem to be forever tripping over themselves.

Don't let the façade of bravado fool you. The too-tall or too-short boy may make jokes about his size, but it's tough to be different from the rest of the crowd. The underweight or overweight teen-age girl may seem cheerful but you can take my word for it, she suffers silently. I receive many letters from adolescents who cry on my shoulder because they are ashamed to let anyone else know how they feel. This letter from Portland, Maine, tells a typical story:

"I'm a girl, fifteen, and so miserable I can't describe my feelings. I put on a jolly front but inside I die. My mother is petite, like a little China doll. My Dad was a tackle at Notre Dame. With my lousy luck I had to be built like him instead of her. I'm not fat, I'm just big.

"The problem is my grandmother who lives with us. Whenever anybody comes to the house she says 'How old do you think Marcia is? Take a guess.' Of course they guess about nineteen or twenty and I feel like crawling under the rug. I have asked Grandma a hundred times please not do this to me any more, but she only smiles and says 'Don't be so touchy, child!' The other evening she did the same thing in front of about eight people. She asked everyone to 'take a guess.' I got so mad I couldn't control myself so I said to one of the men 'Now how old do you think Grandma is?' He answered 'About eighty.'

Well, Grandma is seventy-one and she was furious. She marched right into the library where my dad was doing some book work and told him what I had said. Then she told my mother. They both said I should apologize. Do you think I should, Ann?"

The letter was signed "The Moose." I replied:

"Apologize. And if Grandma hasn't learned her lesson, say it again and then apologize again. Your grandmother does not understand the agony of children who are large for their age. Calling attention to your physical size is cruel—particularly when you have repeatedly asked her not to. You should be permitted to protect yourself as best you can."

In the years between fourteen and seventeen your teen-ager is likely to be most critical of you. The hostility is often open, and there may be "I hate Mother" and "I hate Father" days. If you can understand what is behind this hostility, it will help you to live through some dark moments.

When a child says "I hate you," he hates himself, too. He is unhappy and frustrated. His feelings of conflict are bewildering and frightening to him. Teen-agers are eager for independence but they are afraid of it, too. They want more freedom but they aren't certain they can handle it. They insist they want to be let alone to "run their own lives" but they are often fearful of leaving the nest.

The following letter catalogues a good many of the teen-age gripes against parents:

"I have two problems—my mother and my father. They are driving me nuts. They don't realize that I am a grown woman of fifteen. They want to know who is on the phone every time it rings. They want to know the life history of every fellow I go out with. They want to know where I'm going every time I step my foot outside the house. Mother says I'm still a child—until there is work to be done—then suddenly I'm an adult. She's on my back every minute about something or other. My dad acts as if going steady was a crime or something. I've talked myself hoarse on the subject but they don't seem to understand that we are living in a different century than when *they* grew up. I need more freedom and I wish you would help me out by putting this letter in the paper so they can see it. And please hurry your answer. I think I'm cracking up."

This letter puts a spotlight on the most tormenting question facing parents of teen-agers—how much freedom should I give my child? The question is particularly difficult because there is no easy formula, no pat answer.

Some girls at thirteen are wonderful baby sitters; others at thirteen need a baby sitter themselves. I have known fifteen-year-old boys who handle a car with more skill and judgment than their mothers. Other boys at seventeen are so juvenile and erratic that it's criminal to let them sit behind the wheel even when they're accompanied by an adult.

The question of the measure of freedom and independence you give your teen-ager must be determined by a dispassionate evaluation of what your teen-ager is like. I don't mean what he *says* he's like or what you *wish* he were like—I mean his record of performance. How does he handle his responsibilities and obligations? Does he help with the work around the house without feeling abused? Does he do the job in school? Is he responsible about the family car—or do mysterious dents appear in the fender? Does he return it with the gas tank empty, the battery run down and the tires low? Is your teen-ager reliable and truthful? Does she respect the curfew you have set for her—or do you pace the floor at night, worried sick because she should have been home hours ago? Does she take care of her clothes or does she leave skirts on the chair, blouses on the floor, forget to mend what is ripped—then beg to borrow yours when she's in a hurry and wants to "look nice."

Children should be brought up to feel that they are important. They should know that you love them and that they are precious to you, but they should know, too, that the world is not spinning on its axis for them alone. They should be taught that all members of the family are expected to give as well as take.

I have a pretty good idea of what goes on when a father writes:

> "Our teen-agers act as if they are living in a hotel. They never do a lick of work. They check in and out when they please and sometimes stay overnight with friends and forget to tell us. Their mother is expected to have all their clothes pressed and ready to put on at a moment's notice. Our daughter got mad at me yesterday because I failed to take a telephone message properly. I didn't get the boy's last name. How did I know she was dating three fellows named Jack?"

Teen-agers should be taught that they will be given privileges in direct ratio to their ability to assume and execute responsibilities. Let them know that freedom must be earned. A thirteen-year-old girl who must be told to wash her neck, practice the piano, and write those thank-you notes which are two months overdue should not be allowed to have her own telephone and go to the movies on Saturday. The general idea is this: If you want to be treated like an adult, then act like one. Maturity is measured by a teen-ager's capacity to discharge his obligations without having to be threatened, nagged, humored, or hit over the head.

All parents should allow their teen-agers to make a great many decisions for themselves. The vital question is where to draw the line. But wherever the line is drawn, remem-

ber that even a foolish decision can be a useful one if the
teen-ager learns a lesson from the mistake. Just take care that
you don't bail your teen out of every embarrassing or awkward situation. The advice worked for this Buffalo mother:

> "No problem, Ann, just a note to thank you for your
> advice and to let you know it worked. Remember last April
> when our seventeen-year-old son wanted to buy a broken
> down jalopy for $300? He had saved the money from odd
> jobs and Grandma's Christmas checks. We told him the
> car might cost a lot to keep up because it was in pretty bad
> shape and would be needing repairs. He insisted that the
> money was his and that he ought to be free to spend it as
> he saw fit. So he bought the car and Dad and I never
> said a word. After three months the engine needed a new
> block and three tires were shot. He announced at dinner
> last night that the car was sure a bad bargain and he would
> be lucky if he got $30 out of junking it. Nobody said I
> told you so (and I'm sure *he* appreciated that) but the
> lesson was clear. Dad and I were delighted that he learned
> it first hand. Thank you for advising us to let him learn
> this one the hard way."

Another letter—same lesson, feminine angle—came from
Augusta, Maine:

> "This may not seem important to you but I need your
> advice fast. It's almost a matter of life and death in our
> house and I don't know what to do. Three months ago
> our sixteen-year-old daughter was given permission to select
> her own winter coat. She shopped for several hours on a
> Saturday afternoon and then brought home two coats and
> asked me to help her decide. One coat was a flashy white
> leather number with patch pockets and a tie-over belt.
> The other one was a navy blue wool, conservative and
> with simple lines. I told her the navy wool would be more
> practical because she could wear it for both sport and
> dress. She said maybe I was right, but the white coat

would be such a knockout at football games that she just couldn't pass it up. So, she bought the white coat. That was three months ago. Last night she came to me in tears. She has been invited to a dress-up party a week from Saturday night and she has no coat to wear. The white leather coat is a little cracked and it has turned a bit gray. It's too sporty to wear over the silk dress—they just don't look right together. She wants to buy a new coat and this time she is willing to let me select it. What shall I do?"

Time was short, so I wired her:

"Don't cave in. Let her wear the white leather coat. Next fall let her make her own selection again. I'll bet she'll buy a navy wool."

A white leather coat over a silk dress or $300 spent on a bucket of bolts will make little difference in later life, but there are some mistakes which we should not allow our children to make because they are too costly. When your teen-ager wants to do something that you feel could do permanent damage say no—and mean it. Parents must not allow themselves to be cowed or out-maneuvered. Too many so-called adults fold up under pressure. Their children nag them into saying yes after they've already said no. Children learn early if a concentrated campaign of pleading will result in a reversed verdict. Experience teaches them whether or not they have "collapsible" parents. One fifteen-year-old Dayton girl wrote "If I don't get what I want I just stop eating. It never fails to do the trick."

One of the most damaging decisions a teen-ager can make is quitting school to take a job. The young person who is eager to earn money does not realize that leaving school to earn $55 a week may sentence him permanently to the $55 level. By the time he knows the score it may be too late to go back to school and pick up where he left off.

Allowing children to plunge into boy-girl activities too soon is another serious mistake. They have no way of knowing how much fun they miss in their early years by trying to reach out for premature adulthood. Sixth and seventh graders can't possibly know of the temptations that may come their way if they are allowed to go off in pairs and are left to their own devices. The sight of a thirteen-year-old boy in a dinner jacket is enough to make me sick. A twelve-year-old girl in a strapless tulle evening gown (which keeps falling down because the poor thing can't fill it) is a pathetic sight.

Girls who start to date at twelve are usually going steady at fourteen. When they've reached the ripe old age of sixteen, they have dated or gone steady with almost every boy of their acquaintance who would ask them out. School seems "dull" after four years of extracurricular excitement so the next step is marriage because there's nothing left that they haven't tried. The following letter is one of my best examples of this sorry state of affairs. It was written by a Columbus, Ohio, mother:

> "Several months ago our daughter who was fifteen started to date a soldier stationed a short distance from here. He is nineteen. They fell in love and she dropped all her other boy friends. When they asked for permission to get married, my husband and I were shocked. We told them they had better wait a year or so. At first they accepted it, but after a few weeks our daughter told us they were so in love we just had to sign for her or she'd have a nervous breakdown. We had a long talk with both of them and we agreed to give them permission, providing our daughter would give us her solemn word that she would stay in school and graduate. They were married two months before her sixteenth birthday.
>
> "Last week she came to us all upset. Her husband is being transferred to Tennessee and he wants her to go

with him. She would have to break her promise and leave school. If we get tough and insist that she keep her promise and stay in school, her husband will be mad. What can we do?"

I told the mother that she and her husband could take turns kicking themselves for allowing a fifteen-year-old girl to marry. The time to have gotten tough was before they were married. Married people belong together. If you think this case is an isolated one, have a statistic: One bride out of every seven in the United States is seventeen years of age or younger.

Teen-agers become expert at wheedling more freedom than they should have by falling back on the age-old phrase "everybody's doing it. I'm the only one in the crowd who can't." The strategy, of course, is to make parents feel guilty by suggesting that their nineteenth century standards are making the youngster look ridiculous. There's only one answer for this: "We don't care about 'everybody.' We care about you. You are our responsibility and we aren't going to let you do things that may jeopardize your future, no matter what the rest of the kids are doing."

The teen-ager may put on a long face and insist that he is being persecuted, but secretly he will be pleased that you love him enough to be firm. It would be a whole lot easier to say yes to everything—and your teen-ager knows it.

All children feel more secure if there is positive direction. The delinquent and non-productive teen-ager often goes wrong because no one ever demanded that he do certain things in a specific manner. These unfortunate ones grow up unable to stick to principles. Their disregard for authority often leads them to failure in school and sometimes to trouble with the law.

Parental respect has taken a whale of a beating in the

past 25 years. I do not believe that children should be terrified of their parents (as some of us were) but neither should the parents be terrified of their children. Free exchange of opinion is healthy and it contributes to an honest relationship, but there should be reasonable ground rules. If you as parents have a difficult time deciding what those rules are, I recommend that you give yourselves the edge for a change; your children will take the edge whenever *they* can. It's better to be a shade too firm than a shade too lenient.

Nonetheless, if you expect consideration and respect from your children, you must give it. Children have rights and you must acknowledge those rights and respect them. The following exchange illustrates the point:

> "I am so mad at my mother I could just do something terrible. Today when I was in school she went into my desk drawer and read my diary. It was locked but she somehow jimmied it open. There were some very personal things in there that I didn't want anyone to know about. Tonight after supper Mother began to ask me some odd questions. I knew something was wrong. When I went to write in my diary I noticed that the lock was scratched and it had been opened. I accused her outright and she said a girl who had nothing to be ashamed of wouldn't be afraid to let anybody look at her diary. I have lost all respect for my mother. I think she is an underhanded sneak. She says *I* am the one who is wrong, not her. What do you think about this? Does a mother have the right to go into her daughter's diary?"

I devoted an entire column to this letter and my response because I had had the question put to me so many times. The answer I gave was an emphatic *no*. A diary is the personal property of the writer and this was clearly an invasion of privacy.

The column was greeted with warm letters from grateful teen-agers. One girl from San Jose wrote: "I can't afford to send you flowers, which is what you deserve for that wonderful answer, but here's a picture." On a separate sheet of paper was a drawing of a lovely bouquet. Of course, there was some angry reaction from mothers. The most vitriolic letter came from Memphis:

"So you don't think mothers should look in their daughters' diary? Well, how else can we find out what our daughters are up to nowadays? That little tramp of mine tells me she's going one place and then she goes some place else. Her word isn't worth a nickel. She doesn't tell me who she is going with or what she is doing. If I didn't read her diary I wouldn't know anything. Mothers know better than you what is good for their daughters. So why don't you mind your own business?"

I told the embittered mother that if she must snoop in her daughter's diary to find out what's going on, their relationship is in sad shape. I suggested she get outside help. A third party (someone the daughter respected) should be called in to mediate the war.

Teen-agers have a strong sense of justice. They can tolerate stern disciplinary measures if they feel you are fair. Respecting their privacy gives them a sense of self-esteem. It also demonstrates that you have personal integrity. A parent should not open a teen-ager's mail, listen in on the extension telephone or go through bureau drawers in search of clues to his behavior.

Even little signs of respect are important. If you don't want your teen-ager to barge into your bedroom without first knocking, then give him the same courtesy. Say "thank you" and "please" when you want him to do something. Don't order him—ask him. If you use a gentle and friendly approach, he will too. If you snarl and bark, he'll snarl and bark back at you—and at others.

So when you find yourself tempted to use that phrase "When I was your age . . . ," go ahead and use it—but level with your children. Tell them that you didn't win every contest, that you weren't the star of every event. Let them know that you didn't get every fellow you set your cap for. Tell them a few of your most humiliating experiences. Describe some of your failures. It will make you seem more human and they will love you for it. No one can be the soul of perfection 24 hours a day—so don't try to suggest you managed it. You'll find your children will be much more honest with you if they feel you are completely honest with them. Nobody wants to take his troubles to someone who has never made a mistake.

If you can say to your teen-ager, "Yes, I know exactly how you feel because I traveled that same road myself and it's rough," he may listen more sympathetically than if you say, "You kids nowadays are just spoiled rotten. I didn't have one half the opportunities . . ." etc. etc. etc.

Your major job as a parent is to equip your child to lead an independent, productive, useful life. Live *with* your child—not *for* him. For the most part, let him take his own lumps but don't let him jump off a cliff to learn first hand what's at the bottom. Be firm but be fair. Respect him and his rights and you won't have to worry about his respect for you.

If you guide your child in the way he should go, he will love life and embrace with enthusiasm its challenges. Recently I had one of the most rewarding days of my life—a day that made me feel that all the effort was worth while. It was my daughter's twenty-first birthday. She sent me a dozen red roses with one line on the enclosed card: "Thank you for having me."

THIRTEEN

T een-agers and sex

(Note to Parents. Private: Keep Out)

"THESE ARE the happiest days of your life." When I hear an adult say this to a teen-ager I know he has a weak memory. Teen-age years can be the worst. They are the years when you learn some of life's toughest lessons—the hard way.

What battles are you teen-agers fighting? Your letters tell me. Thousands of teens from all sections of the country use the same phrases to describe their misery:

"I'm a flop. I can't do anything right. I'm the most mixed up kid who ever lived."

"My parents are squares. They are ruining my social life. I have to leave parties just when the fun starts. . . ."

"I have a driver's license, but I never get the car because my mother worries. I drive better than she does. . . ."

"My dad smelled cigarette smoke on my breath and you'd have thought I had committed a murder or something. . . ."

"How can I make a very good-looking guy keep his hands to himself? I like him a lot and don't want to lose him, but he's been getting out of line lately. Please hurry your answer. I have to know by Saturday night. . . ."

"My boy friend and I have been going steady for five months. We are trying to control ourselves but I don't know how much longer we will be able to manage."

"I've told you everything. Could I be pregnant? Please answer 'yes' or 'no' in the confidential part of your column. If my mother knew I was asking this question she'd kill me."

I have a pretty good idea of what goes on with you kids. And I should have—because I get my information from the most reliable of all sources: you.

Is it harder to be a teen-ager today than when your folks grew up? I think it is. I remember clearly when I was sixteen (back in the Stone Age, of course) and it was no picnic then. But I believe you kids have an even rockier time. Why? Because you have more freedom, more money to spend, more leisure, more distractions, and more choices to make.

When I was fourteen and my mother said "No," if I asked "Why?" she didn't sit down and tell me about Dr. William Menninger or Sigmund Freud. She gave me a withering look and said "Because I said so!" And that settled it. Maybe I felt she was a little unreasonable, but "No" meant "No" and it was silly to think about that subject any longer.

Today many mothers say "Well, dear, it's up to you . . . ," and suddenly you find yourself burdened with the responsibility of a decision. You know that since the choice is yours, you are also responsible for the consequences. This can be a problem.

If I were asked to name the factor which has had the

greatest influence on teen-age behavior in the past 25 years, I would say it is the automobile. A quarter of a century ago (which is about when your parents were teen-agers) high school boys who had their own cars were as rare as hen's teeth. Some fellows (and almost no girls) were able to borrow the family car, but it had to be a pretty special occasion. Today, almost every teen-ager can get four wheels under him on a moment's notice. A car means more than transportation. It can be a status symbol, an energy outlet and—as you know, a portable bedroom. The majority of teen-agers who write to me about their intimacies confess that the trouble started in a parked car.

A generation ago girls went with the boys they met in school or in church. Generally the boy lived in her neighborhood or no farther away than a bus ride. Today, the automobile has made it possible for fellows to show up from the other end of town, from neighboring counties, suburbs, and even communities a hundred miles away. The girl's parents may or may not know the boy's parents or what kind of fellow he is. He suddenly appears with a car and they drive off together. I'm not saying he's a bad apple—he may be a plum, but when kids have a car they also have the freedom to go wherever they choose and do whatever they wish. If they happen to select a drive-in theater which features a sexy movie, it adds to the hazards.

Or they may be double-dating with a couple who have been necking heavily for quite some time. Suddenly it seems like a good idea, even though they hadn't planned on "that kind" of an evening. Add to this a full moon and a few cans of beer or a pint of bourbon which just happened to be in the glove compartment and you have a tailor-made setup for big trouble.

I have addressed hundreds of high school audiences from Anderson, South Carolina, to La Crosse, Wisconsin—from

New Orleans to Portland, Oregon, and I give a very frank talk. There is no point in wasting my time or the time of the students by pretending they are wide-eyed innocents. Today's teen-agers know plenty. I let them know at the outset that I didn't come to criticize, preach, or threaten them. I'm there to discuss their problems, openly and honestly, and to advise them. My talks are primarily about sex and marriage. I don't think I've ever had a disinterested audience.

When I was in high school I never heard a speech like mine. Even if someone had been willing to speak so frankly, I doubt if the high schools would have permitted it. It was considered a major event in our high school when a big game hunter came with movies of his trip to Africa. The closest thing to sex was a three-second close-up of the native women—bare from the waist up. A few boys invariably giggled or whistled and three or four teachers began combing the audience for the culprits so they could be removed from the auditorium.

Kids in our day were more self-conscious about sex than today's teen-agers. We were every bit as interested (it's fairly obvious the interest has been pretty high since man began), but we weren't as sophisticated as you.

Twenty-five years ago thirteen-year-old girls didn't wear lipstick, nylons, nail polish, or tulle formals. Dating started at about sixteen. Fifteen-year-old boys didn't own dinner jackets and wear cuff links. Did we neck? Of course, but not nearly as early nor as often. There was neither the social pressure to hurry up and grow up, nor was there the stimulation of drive-ins, leisure time, and spare cash. But we *did* neck, and we were pulled and hauled by our inner conflicts just as you are.

What is necking? Let's define our terms. In plain language necking is from the neck up. It is an exchange of kisses and caresses, keeping both feet on the floor and all hands on deck. Is necking wrong? Well, it depends on what it means to you and what it means to the person with whom you are necking.

If you parents happen to be reading this chapter I'll bet your eyes are bugging. You are probably muttering "What's Ann Landers telling our kids anyway—is she saying it's all right to neck?" You are not supposed to be reading this chapter in the first place—it's for teen-agers. And furthermore, if you think your teen-ager isn't going in for a little necking, it's time you woke up and smelled the coffee.

Normal kids neck. I'd worry about a high school senior (boy or girl) who has never been kissed. Now that we've settled *that*, let's get on to some rules to keep the necking under control.

If you are seeing a lot of a certain someone, have a planned program of activity. Don't just sit around with nothing special to do or, even worse, ride around with no destination. Teen-agers should bowl, swim, play tennis, golf, visit museums and art galleries, concerts and sports events. A sensible way to stay out of trouble is to keep active and busy. When necking becomes the major interest and number one indoor sport, you are playing with fire and you could get badly singed.

For this very reason, I'm not in favor of going steady. Young people who spend hours and hours together and go with one another exclusively become too intimate over a period of months or years. It's inevitable. The couples who go steady rationalize their heavy necking because they "belong to each other." It is easy to go a little farther every time they neck. Kids seldom do *less* than they did the last time.

The living room of your own home is the safest place to neck. And there must always be a light on. It goes without saying that a respectable girl never invites a boy into her house unless one or both parents are at home. If parents have good judgment, they will get lost after saying hello and visiting briefly. I am not suggesting that the teen-age daughter take over the living room for the evening. (In fact the boy who comes over night after night to sit on the davenport and raid the icebox is my idea of a creep. He can hardly be called a date.) What I am suggesting is that the teen-age girl invite her very special fellow in after the movie, play, dance, or game. A time limit should be established in advance. Thirty minutes is plenty. A sixteen-year-old girl should be in the house by midnight and the boy should be on his way by 12:30. Dating on school nights, of course, is absolutely out.

And now—what is petting?

Petting is roaming hands, passionate kissing, loose garments (for comfort, of course). Given all this, somehow the feet leave the floor and you gradually become too weak to sit up so you recline. Petting can:

Make you feel guilty and ashamed.

Ruin your reputation.

Cause you to lose your boy friend because after he goes farther than he knows he should, he may decide you're cheap.

Lead to pregnancy.

Break your parents' hearts.

Result in an unwanted marriage or a child out of wedlock.

This letter from Plainfield, New Jersey, describes the plight of a teen-age girl who signed her letter "Finished at sixteen."

> "*Dear Ann Landers:* I'm going out of my mind. Please, please help me. I keep thinking I'll wake up and find it's all a bad dream. But I know better. I started to go steady

with Paul when I was not quite fifteen. He was my first sweetheart and I thought he was the most wonderful guy in the world. He was a year ahead of me in school but we saw each other every day and usually had lunch together. We'd study almost every evening and on Friday and Saturday night we'd do something with the gang, go to a movie or a party or just for a ride.

"We started to neck after about five dates. Paul had a second-hand convertible and we used to drive to a secluded little spot. After these necking sessions I would feel half wonderful and half miserable. He kept telling me there was nothing wrong with it when two people loved each other. I tried to believe him, but somehow I felt ashamed. Last May after the Junior Prom, he had a few drinks and so did I. We went off to our secluded little spot and it happened.

"It was as if a big ocean wave had swept me off my feet. Paul said he loved me more than ever because I was 'his.' I was so mixed up that night I don't think I slept a wink. Well, once you go all the way, you just can't help yourself after that. He'd come to the place where I was baby sitting or over to my house—or his house—wherever we were sure we'd have a place to ourselves for a couple of hours.

"We talked about getting married and he always said it would be a long way off because he had four years of college ahead of him and then engineering school. Well, Ann, to get to the point of this letter, I am about three months pregnant. I haven't been to a doctor but I'm sure. I told Paul when I first suspected it and do you know what he said? 'Gee, that's a tough break. I can't afford to get mixed up in this. My old man would have a fit. I'll have to deny it if you say I'm responsible.'

"I see Paul at school every day and he ducks around corners. I hate the very sight of him now and I wouldn't marry him even if he begged me. A few nice fellows have asked me out now that they know Paul and I aren't going steady, but how can I accept dates knowing what is happening to me?

"I can't concentrate on my school work and my grades are slipping. I feel half sick and nervous all the time wondering if anybody suspects. My skirts and blouses are getting tight and my mother says I look pale and that I don't seem like myself lately. Please, Ann, is there any place I can go? Will it cost much? How soon would they take me? Please send the information as soon as possible. It will make it easier if I know these things when I tell my folks—and I've got to tell them right away. Thank you for any help you can give me."

If you teen-age girls think this happens only to the cheaper types, you're wrong. I have visited homes for unwed mothers in a good many cities and some of the girls I met were dolls—and from fine families, too. It doesn't happen only to tramps. In fact, the theory has been advanced that the tramps don't often get into this kind of trouble because they are experienced and know how to prevent it.

When I addressed a conference of teen-agers in Toledo a young girl rose from the audience to ask this question: "Why do you direct your comment on moral behavior to us girls? Don't you feel that the fellows have an equal responsibility to keep their emotions in check?"

I replied, "Because girls get pregnant."

The cold, hard facts of life—however unpretty they may sound—are these:

Most boys will go as far as they can. They'll take anything that is offered plus whatever they can talk a girl into giving. Boys are more easily aroused than girls and their sexual demands are likely to be of a more urgent and insistent nature. A teen-age boy is concerned primarily with his biological drives and not with "love." And to be blunt, a boy doesn't have much to lose.

In the olden days (back in the 1930s) the pitch was "Be

good because virtue is its own reward." Words like "virtue" and "chastity" are not important in today's teen-age vocabulary. These words suggest thin-lipped, strait-laced spinsters in choker pearls and red velvet. I don't know that it has ever been tried, but I'm willing to bet if the words "chastity" and "virtue" were included in a psychological word-association test, the overwhelming majority of teen-agers would link them with Queen Victoria. The slogan "Be good because virtue and chastity are beautiful" doesn't hold much appeal nowadays.

So, I'd like you teen-age girls to try this one for size: "Be good because it's smart. You have too much to lose if you play it the other way." The girl who has respect for herself considers her body personal property. It belongs to her. She is responsible for what happens to it. She doesn't let a boy use her as a plaything.

Some girls who write say they go further than they should because they're afraid the fellows won't ask them out a second or third time if they don't defrost a little. It is not true that the "make-outs" are popular and that the well-behaved girls sit dateless. The fireball may get a fast play for a limited time, but when the word gets around, the girl is considered neither respectable nor desirable. She is just "available."

A good many disappointed mothers write to me about this. Here is such a letter from Indianapolis:

> "My daughter is seventeen and hasn't had a date in over eight months. I think it's a shame that a lovely, well-mannered, bright girl like Rosalie sits home night after night while the cheap girls in town are rushed to death. When she told me the reason, I was shocked. What's wrong with this generation of young boys that they refuse to take out a girl unless they can count on a hot necking session?"

I told the mother her daughter was not giving her the straight goods. Boys always have—and still do—like girls who are interesting and good conversationalists (which usually means good listeners). Boys enjoy dating girls who are fun and can contribute something to the group. Looks help, but they are not all-important. Some of the most beautiful girls in town can be the loneliest—while the plain Janes may have scads of dates.

The girl who behaves herself has peace of mind. She's free of the agonizing fears which torment her foolish sisters who have overstepped the bounds. Here are a few excerpts from the mail pinpointing those fears:

> "I'm scared to death my mother suspects what I've been doing. I can't look her straight in the eye. . . ."

> "I'm not going with Jerry any more. There was a lot of bitterness when we broke up. I'm afraid he'll tell. . . ."

> "I went too far and now I'm sorry. I don't want to keep on this way but I'm afraid he'll quit me if I refuse him. . . ."

> "I'm almost out of my mind with worry. I think I'm pregnant. . . ."

By this time, girls, if you haven't got the idea, here it is in one sentence: Sex outside of marriage isn't worth the fear, the guilt, the loss of reputation, the anxiety, and the risk of pregnancy.

And now, a word to you teen-age boys: A great many of you subscribe to the sophism that sex is natural so why not enjoy it. I'm not so naive that I think I can change your approach to girls, but here are a few thoughts to kick around.

Of course sex is natural. So is eating. But would you sit down at the dinner table and pull the leg off a turkey or scoop the mashed potatoes up with your hands? Would you grab the fresh rolls off a bakery counter and stuff them into your mouth? Of course not, because civilized people are expected to control their natural instincts. This distinguishes men from beasts.

The civilized person disciplines himself. He isn't a slave to his impulses. He exercises judgment, respects the rights of others, and weighs the consequences of his behavior. The following letter shook me. What do you think of it?

"I'm not writing for advice. It's too late for that now. I just hope you'll print this letter. Perhaps it will help someone else. Our youngest son is eighteen. He should be graduating from high school in June, but he won't. He was married three weeks ago to a girl who is sixteen. They are expecting a baby in October.

"Betty and Al went together three months. She seemed like a pleasant girl, but quite shy. Her parents are divorced and her mother works downtown. Al never brought her over to the house the way he did other girls—and he never talked much about her. One day I asked him casually where his class ring was and he said Betty had it. I asked him if he had a crush on Betty and he replied 'She's all right.' His lack of enthusiasm made me uneasy.

"It was a month ago today that Betty's mother phoned and suggested I come over that evening and bring my husband. I sensed trouble and refused to get off the phone until she told me more. When she said 'Betty and Al had better get married right away,' I knew the whole story. That night when my husband came home from the office I told him. We didn't eat much dinner, just went right over to Betty's house. We took Al with us.

"It was the most horrible evening of my life. Al sat there with his head buried in his hands and Betty cried the whole time. Betty's mother tried to be helpful. She offered Betty and Al her bedroom and said she'd take the pull-out bed in the living room. It broke my heart when she said 'Betty will need someone to help her care for

the baby. She doesn't know a thing. She's just a baby herself.'

"So our eighteen-year-old son had to quit high school
and marry a sixteen-year-old girl. He had planned on going
to college—even had a football scholarship lined up but
that's out the window now. We begged him to stay in
school but he said he couldn't face the kids.

"The worst part of it is I don't think he cares much for
this girl. They look so sad together. I don't know whether
it's our fault for not teaching our son better, or the girl's
fault, or her mother's. But at this stage, fixing the blame
doesn't help much. Please, Ann, keep alerting these young
kids to the dangers of going too far. Tell the boys that if
the girls tease and egg them on, they should think beyond
the pleasures of the moment. One foolish mistake can
mean a ruined life for both of them.

A Mother"

So, what can teen-agers do to stay out of trouble—

Girls: You can avoid temptation by steering clear of situations which can easily lead to unrestrained love-making.
This means no parking in cars. If you want to neck, go
home. With your parents in the house you aren't likely to
go farther than you should. If your parents don't impose a
curfew on your visiting boy friends, impose a curfew
yourself. Half an hour is plenty.

Boys: Don't sit around and look at smutty magazines
and read junk that fires your imagination and stimulates
you sexually. Channel your energies into constructive outlets. Go out for football, basketball, or baseball. Play tennis, golf, ping-pong, soccer or handball. Improve your
swimming, wash the car, paint the garage, practice the
trombone, build a boat, do your homework, mow the lawn,
clean the attic. *Keep busy.*

Boys and girls: Stay away from liquor. I have never heard

of liquor doing teen-agers any good. I've had stacks of letters, however, from high school students who have confessed that if they hadn't had so much to drink, they might have avoided trouble.

Alcohol does strange things. It anesthetizes part of your brain. Do you know that numb feeling you get when the dentist gives you a shot of novocain? Well, alcohol acts the same way. Your vision is affected, your coordination is off, and your personality changes. That part of your brain which acts as a censoring agent is inoperable. You suddenly hear yourself saying things you would not ordinarily say. Liquor loosens the tongue and fogs the judgment.

Often when people drink they imagine they are articulate, witty, amusing, even brilliant. They think they can sing better and dance better. These are illusions soaked in spirits. Alcohol has never been known to improve talent or bring out hidden genius. It only plays little tricks on your brain.

Many teens who become involved in sexual adventures say they had had too much to drink or it wouldn't have happened. This is more than likely because liquor removes inhibitions and destroys will power. Teen-agers who tell me they have to drink to be part of the crowd get this answer: "You need a new crowd."

You teen-agers have your lives ahead of you. It can be a glorious adventure filled with the excitement of achievement, the satisfaction of service and the joy of reflecting favorably on those who love you.

You must choose the way you will go and accept responsibility for yourself. You have the information and you know the score. You can play it right—or you can louse things up. No one is going to follow you around to keep you out of trouble. The best chaperone is your own conscience.

FOURTEEN

The battle of the bottle

"Oh, God, that men should put an enemy in
their mouths to steal away their brains!"
                                        Shakespeare

I AM AGAINST excessive drinking, and this fact is well-
known to those who read the Ann Landers column. I
am not, however, a Carry Nation who is trying to dry up
the world. I know that not everyone who takes a highball
is headed for the gutter or cirrhosis of the liver. Some
people can take it or leave it alone. But, unfortunately,
millions of Americans are taking it when they *should* be
leaving it alone.

Some people feel that they need alcohol to lift their
spirits, settle their nerves, put them at ease, help them escape from reality, sharpen their wits or blunt them so that

they can tolerate people who drink. As for me, I prefer lemonade. This, of course, doesn't make me any better or any worse than anyone else.

Many readers applaud my stand and others have called me a "Bluenose," a "Prohi," and just plain hipped on the subject. A Tulsa reader wrote:

> "I wish you'd stop beating the subject to death. Your incessant hammering on the evils of liquor is making you sound like a nut. My husband and I enjoy a couple martinis before dinner. We've never seen a pink elephant, hit a light pole, been evicted from a night club or had a hangover that wasn't gone by noon. So why don't you button your lip?"

She signed herself "Moderate Mixer."

I told "Moderate Mixer" that perhaps liquor was no problem to her, or to her husband, but that millions of Americans were fighting (and losing) a daily battle with the bottle. I promised to continue to harp on the subject until my typewriter falls apart. The following day's mail brought many letters from readers who offered to buy me a new typewriter.

The diagnosis of alcoholism as a disease rather than a moral deficiency is not new. Whether it should be considered a separate disease or a symptom of some underlying disturbance, either psychological or physiological in origin, is still debated. Even though alcoholism may be considered a symptom of another problem, it is so destructive in its effects that the symptom itself must be dealt with irrespective of the causes.

Statistical studies recite figures placing the number of alcoholics in the United States at from 4.5 to 7 million people. But this does not include uncounted multitudes of drunks who avoid detection for many years—even by their own families—the kitchen drinkers and the bath-room nippers who fill cough medicine bottles with bour-bon and pour gin into hot water bags. The National Coun-cil of Alcoholism estimates that every day approximately 1,000 Americans cross the line that divides the social drinker from the alcoholic. The statistic that most dra-matically makes the point, however, is this: In the United States five billion dollars is spent on liquor every year.

More important than the billions of dollars and the mil-lions of man hours lost to industry is the tragic waste of brilliant minds and able bodies, the warping of what might have been lovely personalities, the shattered ambitions, wrecked dreams, broken homes, neglected children, and the loss of human dignity.

Although I have heard and read many definitions of an alcoholic, I think Dr. Seldon O. Bacon, director of the Yale University Center, said it best:

"If almost all of the people who drink (some 75 mil-lion over the age of fifteen) can control their drinking and the alcoholic can *not*—then this is the clear-cut distinction." Dr. Bacon points out that many an alcoholic considers him-self a social drinker when he is no more a social drinker than a kleptomaniac is a paying customer or an arsonist is a boy scout.

The search for the "authentic alcoholic personality" has been in vain. Alcoholics are found in every walk of life, at every intellectual level, in every income group, among the very young and the very old. There are alcoholic doctors, lawyers, judges, actresses, clergymen, artists, journalists, call girls, high school students, scrub women, panhandlers, and presidents of big corporations.

Even animals can become alcoholic. I once received a letter from a mother who wanted to know what to do about her son who had recently returned from the Navy.

He insisted on putting beer in their airedale's water pan. The mother asked the boy to stop but he replied, "It won't hurt him. In fact he seems to like it." And indeed he *did* like it. After several days of lapping up Budweiser, the airedale turned up his nose at the water which Mother poured in his pan. He sat by the refrigerator for hours and cried for beer. When the dog developed a severe case of hiccups the woman wrote to me for help.

I checked with a veterinarian and learned that animals can develop a taste for intoxicants, that they experience the same apparent exhilaration as humans and that they can also exhibit the same symptoms of inebriation. They become dizzy, fall down, walk into objects and often become ill or fall asleep.

No one knows why one person is an alcoholic and the next person is not. Some specialists insist it is an allergy. Others say it is a glandular malfunction. One school of thought holds that alcoholism is hereditary. Dr. Róger J. Williams of the University of Texas believes that the alcoholic has a congenital need for unusual amounts of certain food elements. A diet which fails to satisfy this need produces a craving for drink. Another theory is that certain emotions, such as resentment, jealousy, and insecurity manufacture chemicals in the body which, when combined with alcohol, destroy the will and the person is no longer in control of himself.

All authorities agree that the alcoholic is sick and needs help. He is just as sick as the consumptive or the cardiac patient. They agree, too, that excessive drinking is triggered by a need to escape. It is a means of anesthetizing the brain against reality. Alcohol eases, for a time at least, the pain of loneliness, failure, grief, and self-hatred. The alcoholic usually is too immature to face up to his responsibilities. He may be an intellectual giant, but he is an emotional midget. When he drinks himself into a stupor, he is in effect saying: "I don't like me or what I have done with my life. I don't want to meet my problems because they are too big for me to handle. I will get drunk and run away from everything. Besides, if I am drunk, I must be forgiven because I am not responsible for what I do or say."

Some psychiatrists say the alcoholic is attempting to destroy himself one day at a time, either because he lacks the courage to put a gun to his head or because he has religious scruples about suicide.

According to Dr. Ruth Fox, medical director of the National Council on Alcoholism in New York, one out of five alcoholics in America is a woman. These housewives who "cook with sherry" somehow have the notion that if it isn't in a shot glass it doesn't count. Some of these women can kill a fifth before Jack gets home for dinner. Only a small percentage of such alcoholics frequent bars or land in jail for disorderly conduct. Most of them are kitchen drinkers who sip themselves into a state of fantasy—usually when no one is watching. The beds go unmade, the dishes stack up in the sink and the children are told that mother has headache spells or gall bladder trouble.

Many people who write to me about marriage problems mention liquor as one of the principal sources of trouble. Men who are married to alcoholic wives are infinitely more sympathetic than women who complain about drinking husbands. Seldom will a husband write: "If she doesn't quit drinking I'm going to throw her out of the house." Most husbands say, "Please tell me what I can do to help her. The kids need a mother."

The family doctor is the best source of advice for a man who has an alcoholic wife. Since the highest hurdle is persuading an alcoholic woman to admit she needs professional help, the visit to the family doctor is a face-saving device. In such cases I suggest to the husband that he make an appointment with the family doctor when his wife complains of not feeling well, then tip him off about the real problem. Most doctors don't need to be clued in, since they are familiar with the symptoms.

If the family has the means, the doctor may suggest private institutional care. (Such care is expensive and therefore impractical for most people.) Or he may suggest psychotherapy. Or he may prescribe a drug which makes the patient violently ill if he drinks liquor when he is taking the medicine. He may suggest Alcoholics Anonymous or some other organization. In any event, the family doctor is usually best equipped to help a husband who finds himself burdened with an alcoholic wife.

How to spot an alcoholic

Many alcoholics can be recognized at a glance by their watery eyes, their blotchy skin—sometimes florid, sometimes ashen. The alcoholic often has enlarged veins on or near the nose. His cheeks sometimes have a tiny network of ruptured blood vessels. His breath may smell of alcohol or perhaps of mints—used to camouflage the alcohol scent. However, alcoholics in the early stages may appear to be perfectly healthy, because physical deterioration hasn't yet set in.

Dr. Seldon O. Bacon in the Kiplinger magazine *Changing Times* listed some guideposts to detect the alcoholic. If you recognize yourself below, you'd better begin to run scared.

1. He begins to drink more than other guests at the same affair.

2. He begins to drink more frequently than others in his group, using feeble excuses.

3. He shows more of the sort of behavior that is ordinarily forbidden, but tolerated at some social drinking functions. Moreover, he is likely to invent behavior-loosening license where none exists.

4. He begins to experience frequent blackouts of memory.

5. He ignores the group's ordinary drinking rules and over-rationalizes his own drinking.

6. He gulps his drinks rapidly, especially at the beginning of a drinking session.

7. He begins to sneak extra drinks.

8. With increasing frequency he drinks to the point of intoxication. He loses control over the amount he drinks —and when and where.

9. He begins experimenting with new patterns, such as switching from bourbon, say, to vodka, drinking only at home or only after 5:00 p.m. He may change his drinking locale, usually finding new companions among people of inferior status. He may become a "loner."

10. He avoids all discussion of alcoholism and produces alibis and lies when forced to discuss it.

11. He may begin to drink in ways unheard of to the nonalcoholic. For instance, he may start the day with seven or eight drinks or go on long weekend binges. He may skip ice, glasses, chasers, and mixers. He may resort to canned heat or vanilla extract.

12. His character and behavior, even when sober, undergo changes, and he may become quarrelsome, dishonest, and self-deceiving.

13. In the final stages there are many manifestations, such as compulsive hiding and storing of drinks against

future hangovers. Unless treated, premature death may end the struggle.

When the husband is alcoholic, the family suffers socially, mentally, financially, and sometimes physically. The following excerpts from my mail illustrate the wide range of problems brought on by excessive drinking:

> "When he drinks, he's brutal to me and the children. He uses vulgar language and sometimes slaps them or me and breaks up the furniture. . . ."

> "Yesterday was pay day and he didn't come home until after midnight. He had less than $4.00 in his pocket. The rent is due on Monday and we owe the milkman. I can't go to my folks again for money. . . ."

> "I found lipstick all over his shirt and handkerchief. When he drinks, he always get mixed up with tramps who hang around bars. He says he docsn't remember being with anybody. . . ."

> "Our teen-age daughter has refused to allow her boy friend to pick her up at home after what happened last night. Her father was drunk and made a terrible scene in front of the boy. He accused him of all sorts of immoral things. She broke into tears and begged the boy to leave. . . ."

> "I had to call Harry's boss this morning because he couldn't get his head off the pillow. I made the excuse that he had a backache and wouldn't be in until later in the day. The boss said he knew all about those backaches and if Harry had one more hangover he was through. . . ."

The millions of American women who are married to alcoholics are, I think, faced with the most challenging of all marital problems. It requires understanding, courage, moral strength and saintly patience to live with an alcoholic. Since alcoholism is a degenerative disease unless treated, the patient gets worse as times goes on. A shocking number of women who write to me have no idea of how to cope with the problem. They don't know what to do so they follow their instincts and treat the alcoholic husband as if he were a spoiled child or a miserable wretch who gets drunk to make life difficult for those around him.

I have kept a list of techniques employed by women who are married to alcoholics. In their well-meaning way they say, "I must do this to keep things going." I tell these women that their intentions may be good but that coddling, fighting, covering up and carrying the total load for a drunk does not help restore him to a normal life. All that these wives manage to "keep going" is the drinking. If you recognize yourself when you read the list below, please heed the advice which follows:

1. If you make excuses for his drinking by blaming his boss, his friends, his job or his war experiences . . .

2. If you go to work to support the family and give him spending money to keep up appearances . . .

3. If you encourage him to drink at home so that he can be watched and not become involved with the law . . .

4. If you send the children on a tour of the gin mills to bring him home . . .

5. If you call up the bar and beg the bartender to throw him out . . .

6. If you pour the liquor down the sink to show him "what you think of it . . ."

7. If you refuse to sleep with him if he doesn't stop drinking . . .

8. If you charge him with assault and battery when he beats you, then withdraw the charges and let him do it again . . .

9. If you refuse to cook for him when he comes home late and drunk . . .

10. If you go out with other men because he gets drunk and goes out with other women . . .

11. If you try to pass the responsibility on to the Lord and rely on prayer alone to make him stop . . .

12. If you do nothing constructive, and hope he will drink himself to death . . .

You're on the wrong track if you found yourself on that list. The natural responses to a drunken husband are disgust or pity. Neither is good; both are destructive. The notion that an alcoholic could stop drinking if he had the will power is fallacious. This is like pleading with a polio cripple to throw away his crutches and walk.

To tell a man, "If you love me you'd stop drinking," is like saying to an athlete, "If you cared about personal hygiene you'd stop sweating." The alcoholic hates his drunkenness, he despises himself and he has probably tried to stop, but he can't.

It is impossible to have a decent, rewarding life with an alcoholic. The wife who continues to cover up for an alcoholic husband only prolongs his years of drunkenness. There is just one sensible course of action for the wife of an alcoholic. It is this: Tell him you know he is sick and that he needs help. Offer to stick by him and help him to help himself. If he refuses, get him out of the house, bag and baggage, and tell him to come back only if he is ready to accept help, or get yourself and the children out of the house and let him know where you can be reached when he is ready for treatment.

Where to get help

I strongly recommend Alcoholics Anonymous because of the remarkable job A.A. has done in rehabilitating alcoholics who have tried everything else and failed. A.A. has more than 8,000 chapters in the United States, Canada, and over 80 other countries. There are no dues. Anyone wishing information on A.A. should consult his local telephone book. If the organization is not listed, write to:

> Alcoholics Anonymous
> P. O. Box 459
> Grand Central Station
> New York 17, New York

A.A. believes that an important part of the patient's recovery is the understanding and moral support of the family. Al-Anon is an organization which has grown out of A.A. to educate the family of the alcoholic so they can cope with the problem. Those who wish to contact Al-Anon can do so through the nearest A.A. chapter.

Many clinics for alcoholics are supported by state and local funds. These are listed in the telephone book. Psychiatrists, physicians, and social workers join together in many communities to help the alcoholic and his family. Many large companies have started programs for their employees.

Information about treatment centers can be obtained from your family doctor, clergyman, judge, welfare agency, city health department, and local police department. The National Council on Alcoholism is the nation's best clearing house for information dealing with treatment centers and clinics. The Council assists community representatives in organizing and establishing local clinics and information centers. The Council's headquarters is at 103 E. 103rd Street, New York 29, New York.

To the alcoholic I address these words:

Alcoholism does not come in bottles. It comes in people. If you want to be helped, the first step is to admit that you are powerless against alcohol. Don't fool yourself into thinking you can cut down or control your drinking. You cannot. An alcoholic can't drink "like other people" because he is not like other people where liquor is concerned. His illness makes him different. This is not a sign of stupidity, immorality, or weakness. His lack of will power is a characteristic of the disease, just as red spots are characteristic of measles. There are thousands of people who were once in the same spot, or worse, and they made it back. The road is difficult and torturous but so is the one you are now following, which is also a dead end.

If you are an alcoholic, the odds are that you're breaking the hearts of at least five people—a father, a mother, a wife, a child, and a brother or sister. No one blames you for what you are now. But if you refuse to accept the help that is available, you must bear the responsibility for what you have done to your life and to the lives of those you love. God helps those who help themselves. May God help you.

FIFTEEN

Be bigger than what happens to you

*"Although the world is very full of suffering, it
is also full of the overcoming of it."*

Helen Keller

F I were asked to give what I consider the single most
useful bit of advice for all humanity it would be this:
Expect trouble as an inevitable part of life and when
it comes, hold your head high, look it squarely in the
eye and say "I will be bigger than you. You cannot defeat
me." Then repeat to yourself the most comforting of all
words, "This too shall pass."

Trouble has its own peculiar values. It can be a friend—if
only because it grows us up. There are many kinds of
trouble, but the most common is the trouble we make for
ourselves because of our own stupidity, inexperience, or

lack of self-control. Here is an example from Canton, Ohio:

"I let this man move into my apartment because we figured it was foolish for both of us to be paying rent. He kept promising we'd be married as soon as he could get a divorce. I found out last week that I am pregnant. When I told him, he got mad at me for 'being so dumb.' That night he packed his clothes and moved back with his family. I am so shocked and hurt by his actions I don't know where to turn. I can't go home to my folks. They are terribly strict. My father doesn't even allow anyone to smoke in the house. I have only $60 to my name and I owe some bills. Please, Ann, tell me what to do. I'm going out of my mind."

What can I say to a woman in this predicament? I can tell her the man is legally responsible for her medical care and for the support of the child. I can tell her if she can't afford a lawyer, she should contact Legal Aid. I can direct her to a home for unwed mothers. It would be pointless to suggest she should not have become involved with a married man in the first place. She knows this.

So what do I say? After outlining the alternatives I give her some words of encouragement. What she needs is confidence and the strength to meet the crisis. And I hope that by printing her letter, I may save some other foolish girl from falling into the same trap.

Maintaining self-respect in the face of a devastating experience is of prime importance. To forgive oneself is perhaps the most difficult of life's challenges. Most of us find it immeasurably easier to forgive others. I've received letters brimming with self-recrimination—letters that prove no punishment is so painful as the self-inflicted kind. Here are a few examples:

"I let my boy friend go too far. Now, when he sees me, he looks the other way. I'm so ashamed of myself I could just die."

"I threw a dish towel in my mother-in-law's face. She was trying to be helpful and I lost my temper. How can I look her in the eye again? I hate myself."

"I got caught cheating in a history exam today. All the kids know about it. I could kill myself."

"I'm not used to liquor. I only drink to celebrate something. Last night was my birthday and I got disgustingly drunk. I insulted people, became sick in the car and disgraced myself. I wish I were dead."

I've written this advice thousands of times:

"It's done. Finished. Over. Stop beating a dead horse. There is nothing you can do to change the past. Take heart from the knowledge that something good can result from everything bad that happens if it teaches you a lesson. Profit from it—then forget it."

Most people with normal intelligence learn from experience. Even a white rat will refuse to follow a piece of cheese along a maze if he discovers after a few attempts that the maze leads him into a puddle of cold water. Some humans, unhappily, don't have the common sense of a white rat. They make the same mistakes time after time. To them, experience merely helps them to recognize the mistake when they make it again. My mail is heavy with examples. A St. Louis woman writes:

"I married an alcoholic. He is brutal and I'm scared to death of him. This is the third time I've picked a rotten husband. I knew Steve drank a little, but I had no idea he was a drunk. Why do I have such miserable luck with men?"

Specialists in the field of human behavior tell us that people who repeatedly bring disaster down on their heads are self-destructive. They feel unworthy and they are unconsciously seeking punishment. Professional help must be sought to end this self-flagellation. Experience is, of course, the best teacher, and that's why life is difficult. We get the grade first and the lesson later. But the important thing is to learn the lesson and then get on with the business of living.

As a youngster I was effervescent, outgoing, and I talked too much. I had a talent for saying the wrong thing at precisely the wrong time. By the time I was a high school freshman, I was better able to synchronize my mouth and my brain, but still I made mistakes and tortured myself because of the foolish things I had said.

One day a high school English teacher taught me with a single dramatic act the futility of rehashing the past. As the students filed into her classroom, we noticed on her desk a quart bottle of milk standing in a heavy stone crock.

"This morning," she announced, "I'm going to teach you a lesson that has nothing to do with English, but it has a lot to do with life." She picked up the bottle of milk, crashed it against the inside of the stone crock, and it splintered into small pieces. "The lesson," he said, "is don't cry over spilled milk."

Then she invited us to look at the wreckage.

"I want all of you to remember this," she said. "Would any of you attempt to restore the bottle to its original form? Does it do any good to wish the bottle had not been broken? Does it help to get upset and tell yourself how good the milk might have tasted if this hadn't happened? Look at this mess! You can moan about it forever, but it won't put the bottle back together again. Remember this broken bottle of milk when something happens in your life that nothing can undo."

I've reminded myself of that broken bottle of milk in the stone crock time and time again. It has helped me to stay afloat on stormy waters. And I'm sure it has saved me uncounted time and unmeasured energy. Our bodies take a physical beating when we put ourselves through an emotional wringer. To try to relive the past or undo what has been done—to daydream about opportunities missed is not only foolish, but it's futile.

Omar Khayyám put it eloquently:

> "The moving finger writes; and having writ,
> Moves on: nor all your Piety nor Wit
> Shall lure it back to cancel half a Line,
> Nor all your Tears wash out a word of it."

Trouble which results from the ill will of others

It would be a wonderful world if all men were honest and decent but they aren't and there's no evidence that they ever will be. We will always be surrounded by liars, crooks, gossips, and bigots—and often they seem to prosper in spite of their tactics. Sometimes it appears that good fortune smiles with special favor on the unconscionable scoundrel who climbs to success on the broken backs of others. A Cincinnati woman wrote:

> "My husband and I put our life's savings into a business venture. A smooth-talker told us we would make a fortune. This man sold manufacturing equipment and he talked us into starting a small plant. We were to buy the machines from him and he would teach us how to run the business. He even offered to hire an experienced factory manager.
>
> "I could write a book on what happened. The machines broke down and we had to buy new parts which cost

money we hadn't planned on spending. The plant manager he hired turned out to be an alcoholic who stayed home three days a week. My husband and I put in 12 and 14 hours a day at the factory and we worked like slaves. At the end of seven months we were broke and the business was in debt. We mortgaged our home and borrowed $5,000 from my father-in-law. Three months later that was gone, too. The man who talked us into the business offered to buy us out for 10¢ on the dollar. We had no choice. Today that man is running the plant and he's making money hand over fist. We learned he owns four other factories which he took over the same way.

"We've consulted a lawyer but legally the man is on safe ground. My husband has developed high blood-pressure and ulcers. The kids make him nervous, and he hasn't spoken a civil word to me in weeks. What can I do to help him back to a normal life?"

I advised the woman to tell her husband that he wasn't the first person to be cheated and he wouldn't be the last. What the smooth-talker did to her husband was reprehensible but what her husband was doing to himself was worse.

Fortunes are made and lost every day. In 1929 thousands of Americans lost every dollar they possessed when the market crashed. Some businessmen put bullets in their heads or jumped out of office windows. Others made themselves sick with worry. Still others picked themselves up, dusted themselves off and went on. The ability to roll with the punches is what separates the men from the boys, and the women from the girls.

Most of us have been victimized in one way or another by an unscrupulous opportunist. Even the experienced can be taken in by a clever operator. In many instances we can't control what happens to us, but we can control our own reactions to what happens to us. We can stay down for the count and be carried out of the ring or we can take the beating and pull ourselves back to our feet. Sometimes the choice isn't even a conscious one.

Many crises seem insurmountable, but time and again we have seen ordinary people display genius in turning a hopeless situation into something tolerable or even good. There should be a citation for the little guy who manages to keep going when he has every right in the world to crack up.

The possibility of nuclear warfare is the most frightening prospect faced by modern man. It's no small order to live calmly in the knowledge that a lunatic thousands of miles away could push a button and finish us all. But every era had problems which were equally terrifying to the people who faced them. Some frightened souls who spread gloom and doom blame the sorry state of the world for their inability to function when the real problem is within themselves. D. H. Lawrence described this man when he wrote of one of his characters, "poor Richard Lovatt worried himself to death struggling with the problem of himself and calling it Australia."

The high cost of getting even

When Jesus said in Matthew 5:4 "love your enemy," He was not only suggesting that we make life easier for *them* but He wanted to make life easier for us. Some contend that such advice is folly. Why give our enemies good will in return for treachery? Should we not try to crush those who try to destroy us?

By "love your enemy" Jesus did not mean that we should "grapple them to our soul with hoops of steel." He *did* mean that to preserve our own mental and physical well-being we should refuse to allow ourselves to be consumed with hatred or bitterness. We must refuse to give evil people the power to break our spirit, make us physically ill, and perhaps even shorten our lives.

The Chinese saying "We are best to ourselves when we are good to others" is a good rule to follow. Bernard Baruch knew and practiced this philosophy.

"One of the secrets of a long and fruitful life," he said, "is to forgive everybody everything every night before you go to bed."

The expression "I'm worried to death" is more than a figure of speech. You can indeed worry yourself to death. The word "worry" comes from an Anglo-Saxon word which means to strangle or choke. The worrier throttles his creative powers. When he is able to free himself from worry, he thinks better, feels better and performs better. Any doctor will tell you that worry, anxiety, tension, and anger can make you sicker than a virus. As far back as Plato man knew that what took place in his mind produced physical changes in his body.

We are all acquainted with examples of such emotional phenomena. An off-color story can produce a blush. The sight of an accident can cause nausea or fainting. Stage fright can cause a pounding of the heart, excessive perspiration, and butterflies in the stomach.

During the first World War thousands of soldiers were incapacitated because of "shell-shock." Many of the afflicted had never been near a shell. In World War II they called it "battle fatigue," although many of the men stricken had never been in combat. They collapsed and were unable to function because of fear and anxiety.

The expression "nervous breakdown" suggests that the nerves have broken down, but the problem is purely emotional. Organically the nerves are healthy. A doctor on the staff of the Mayo Clinic has said the majority of patients in hospital beds today are there because of illnesses which were psycho-generated. This means the sickness was triggered by an emotional problem. Dr. Robert Stolar, an eminent dermatologist in Washington, D.C., and my chief medical authority, says:

"I see patients every day who suffer from rashes and skin eruptions caused by emotional problems. People who let things get under their skin often break out with something on the skin."

People who are frustrated and discontented often dig or pick at themselves unconsciously. The result is a skin irritation. The stoics who are ashamed to display emotions sometimes develop skin trouble. Dr. Stolar once told a strapping construction worker "Your skin is weeping because you cannot."

Dr. Walter Alvarez says most of the ulcer patients who come to his office "got that way from nerves." When they ask if a change of diet would help, he tells them "It's not what you are eating that's making you sick. It's what's eating you."

So—when you find that someone has "done you wrong," say to yourself "I will not spend one extra minute hating or trying to get even. It's too expensive." Hatred is like an acid. It can do more damage to the container in which it is stored than to the object on which it is poured.

Trouble beyond human control

"I am the master of my fate. I am the captain of my soul." These words by William Henley offer courage to the faint of heart. It's comforting for man to feel that he has the power to chart his own destiny. But it isn't always true. Even though we may lead the good life and fight the good fight we are sometimes tripped up by the process of living. Call it bad luck, fate, or whatever you choose, but man is at the mercy of trouble beyond human control.

Here are some examples:

> "*Dear Ann Landers:* I was crippled by polio when I was three. My left arm is withered and one leg is in a brace. I'm eighteen and have never had a real date."

> "My husband and I lost everything in a flood. We were lucky to get our two children out in time. Our neighbors on both sides were drowned."

> "My husband lost both legs in a milling accident in January. We have four children and it's all I can do to keep them clothed and fed. . . ."

> "My wife and only child died in an automobile accident. I was driving. I don't care if tomorrow never comes. . . ."

The letters usually end on the same note of bewilderment. "Why did this terrible thing happen to me?"

What can I say to the heavy-hearted and the sick of soul? Can I tell them to "forget it"? How foolish! I tell them there are no answers. We must trust in the infinite wisdom and the goodness of a greater power. I remind them of Santayana's advice to those who rant about the injustices of life, "Man is not supposed to understand life but to live it."

To a young bride who wrote to me on the day her twenty-four-year-old husband was buried I replied:

> "If you lived through today, you can live through tomorrow. Your burden will be easier to bear with each passing day. It may be difficult to believe, but I promise you will laugh again and enjoy God's good gifts."

Death and tragedy touch us all sooner or later. When it comes it reminds us of our own frailty—and it makes us all brothers and sisters. Shortly after World War II, I was the chairman of a tea for Gold Star mothers. Some women arrived in chauffeured limousines. Others came on foot, not able to afford bus fare. Some wore mink stoles, others, woolen jackets. Their backgrounds and daily lives couldn't have been more different, but their heartache was the same. As they sat side by side, their differences disappeared. The tragedy each shared united them for a time at least. Never before or since have I seen more dramatic proof that trouble is the great equalizer.

I believe in blind faith. I have known people who have suffered deep personal tragedies and they believe in it, too. But, I also believe in the efficacy of positive action to overcome grief. Time is a healer, but those who help time by using it wisely and well make a more rapid adjustment.

Grief, in part, is self-pity turned inside out. The widow who wails "He was everything to me. How can I go on without him . . ." is crying for herself, not for him. Death is sometimes a merciful release from suffering and misery. The one who survives must struggle with the problem of living.

The mourner who wears his grief interminably eventually isolates himself from his friends. The world may stop for a few hours (or perhaps a few days) to hold a hand or to wipe away a tear, but friends and relatives have problems of their own. Life goes on—and those who refuse to go on with it are left alone to wallow in their solitary misery.

The best prescription for a broken heart is activity. And I don't mean plunging into a social whirl or running off on trips. Too many people try to escape from their heartache by hopping on planes, trains and ships. They succeed only in taking their troubles with them. The most useful kind of activity involves doing something to help others. I have told thousands of despondent people, "Enough of this breast-beating. What will it accomplish? No matter how badly off you are there is someone who is worse off—and you can help him."

I advise parents who have lost a child to take a foster child, or children, into their home. The woman who has an abundance of love to give, and no child of her own to accept it, can find a number of lonesome and love-starved children in hospitals. The secret of successful living is *giving*. There are enormous rewards and satisfactions to be reaped working with new Americans, the blind, the deaf, the crippled, the mentally retarded and the aged. Happiness is like perfume. When you spray it on others you're bound to carry a little of the scent away with you.

Several months ago I visited the beautiful home of a newspaper publisher. He and his wife led me to the library to meet their only child, a cerebral palsy victim in his middle twenties. The boy inherited the facial characteristics of his handsome father, but he was a semi-invalid with a severe speech impediment. It was apparent that he would always need constant care. Meeting the boy for the first time shook me. But the strength of his remarkable parents made me ashamed of my feelings. In one brief sentence the boy's father helped me to understand the philosophy that made it possible for him and his wife to accept their lot. He said, "If God saw fit to make such children, I am happy he sent one to us because we know how to love him."

Parents of retarded children belong to a special society. They all pay the same dues—first shocked disbelief, then heartache, and finally the challenge of adjusting. God seems to give these parents a second pair of eyes for seeing what others cannot see. They develop a saintly patience, a nobility of spirit, and a tenderness of heart reserved for them alone.

Pearl Buck, the mother of a retarded child, wrote:
"I cannot say I am glad my child is retarded. That would
be folly. But I can say with a full heart that my daughter's
handicap has renewed my faith in human beings. Through
her my life has become enriched and my heart kept warm.
I meet parents of retarded children everywhere. In every
crowd there is always at least one who comes forward to
take my hand and whisper 'I have a retarded child, too.'
We look into each other's eyes with instant understanding.
We know."

Helen Hayes played the most challenging role of her
career when her daughter Mary, a talented actress of twenty,
was stricken with polio. Miss Hayes had to give strength to
others at a time when she needed support and courage
herself. She wrote of that experience:

"I went to church every morning to pray, but I had become careless with my religion and had cut God out of my
life. I didn't have the nerve to ask Him to make my
daughter well. I prayed only for understanding. I asked
Him to come into my life and let me reach Him. When
Mary died, I felt that my prayers had not been answered.
But I learned later this experience gave my life meaning
which until then had escaped me. I became a living part of
God's world of people."

Most touching to me is the heroism, the courage and
faith of the average people of the world. Often readers who
write about a problem will add something about their personal lives. I am moved by the magnificent people who
write such lines as "My husband lost his sight shortly after
we married, but we manage beautifully." Or "I've had two
operations for cancer, but I know I'll be able to attend my
son's graduation in June and I'm so thankful for that."

No one knows why life must be so punishing to some of
God's finest creatures. Perhaps it is true that everything

has a price and we must sacrifice something precious to gain something else. The poets and philosophers say adversity, sorrow and pain give our lives meaning—an added dimension. Those who suffer deeply touch life at every point; they drain the cup to the dregs while others sip only the bubbles on top. Perhaps no man can touch the stars unless he has known the depths of despair.

SIXTEEN

Age—it's only a number, Baby!

"Grow old along with me
The best is yet to be—
The last of life for which the first was made."
                                        Robert Browning

READERS frequently confess in letters secret anxieties which they would never talk about. My mail shows that thousands of Americans, particularly women, are haunted by the fear of growing old.

Many who write are panic-stricken at the thought of leaving their twenties behind. More are terrified at the prospect of the Big 40. When people kid about age, more often than not they are kidding from the heart. The old line, "What happens to the years a woman hacks off her age?" and the reply, "Oh, they aren't lost—she just adds

them on to the age of a dear friend"—is a savage illustra-
tion of woman's compulsion to remain young, and to make
her contemporaries appear older.

Jokes aside, however, for many the fortieth birthday is a
traumatic experience. Thirty-nine is the year at which both
men and women seem to get stuck. When I was thirty-nine,
I gave my age as forty. I had known so many women who
lied about being thirty-nine that I wanted no part of it.

When I was nine years old, I thought twenty-five was
middle-aged. Anyone over forty was fossilized and couldn't
possibly be getting any fun out of life. A person fifty was a
museum piece and should be treated with reverence simply
because God had allowed him to live so long. Today my
conception of middle-age is approximately ten years older
than I am right now (forty-three).

James Thurber's comment on age in terms of the American culture is amusing, but it's also the way a great many
see it. Thurber said: "In America, love after forty is obscene,
work after fifty is unlikely, and death before sixty is practically a certainty."

Age is important only to the very young and to the very
insecure. Mature people do not think of themselves (or
others) in terms of how many years they have lived. It's
interesting to go around a room and ask each guest in turn
"What age would you like to be if you had a choice?" I
have yet to hear anyone say he would like to be older. Almost every woman (and some men) wish to be younger.
The mature man and woman wish to be exactly the age
they are.

To the insecure female the passing years mean only fad-
ing beauty and competition from younger women. They
write such lines as:

> "I'm forty-six and afraid. When I glanced in the mirror
> this morning, I realized for the first time that I am no

longer young. I wonder how I appear to my husband who works in an office with chic, attractive career girls. Now that I think of it, he's been having dinner downtown more often than he used to. Do you think perhaps—?"

Worshiping at the shrine of youth is an American aberration which has evolved in the last thirty years. The average American homemaker looks at least ten years younger than her grandmother did at a comparable age because her life is easier. Grandma had to cook on a wood stove and bake her own bread. She washed clothes on a board over a tub. But Grandma didn't mind because the TV commercials had not yet told her that if she wanted to be loved by a man she'd better keep her hands soft as satin and wear a "living" bra. Grandma didn't dread the years —she welcomed them. As her children grew older, her responsibilities decreased. There was more time for relaxation. It was indeed "the last of life for which the first was made."

What is the emancipated American woman doing with the hours of leisure provided by push-button living? Too many of these hours are spent on her hair, her fingernails, her toe nails, her face and her body. She is wearing herself out fighting the battle of the birthdays.

Millions of woman-hours and man-dollars are squandered on rejuvenating processes that don't work. Industries have been built on chin straps, "tissue-rebuilding cremes," and hair tints. The following lines appeared in an advertisement of a leading cosmetic firm:

"Do you realize that a potion exists that may well begin the age of agelessness for women? This formula is filled with counterparts of vital substances found in young skin. What's more, it carries them into the living cells. This cream is dedicated to the exciting woman who spends a lifetime living up to her potential. $15 plus tax."

No creature is so pathetic as the woman who is trying to kid the calendar. The girdled hips, the dyed hair, the mask of make-up and the veined feet perched on backless high heels fool no one. The wise woman knows that by the time she has reached fifty she is either wanted and loved for what she is, or she is not wanted and loved, period. Starvation diets, paint jobs, and dressing in the style of her daughter will not help her.

The American ideal of the beautiful woman is a national disgrace. It shrieks of immaturity. Our European sisters have a far more sophisticated approach to age. The European male believes that a woman is not interesting until she is over thirty-five. She doesn't know enough.

When it was suggested to Ethel Barrymore as she approached fifty-five that perhaps a little facial surgery would insure a wider selection of romantic roles, she replied, "Part with my wrinkles—never! They are my credentials for living. I've earned them all."

Discarded wives sometimes write "He left me for a younger woman." In many cases this should be translated into "He left her for a more *interesting* woman." Here is an example of such a letter. Her signature was "Defeated by Youth," but her name is Legion.

> "I was married at twenty. Wally was twenty-three. We were so much in love. We celebrated our twenty-third wedding anniversary in May. Our two children are now in college. Wally has done extremely well financially. To the casual observer we are an ideal couple.
>
> "I thought our marriage was as solid as the Rock of Gibraltar, but last night I got the shock of my life. He told me he's been in love with another woman for two years and wants his freedom so they can be married.
>
> "The other woman is fifteen years younger than I am. I've met her and she is very pretty. There's no use kidding

myself, Ann, I lost out to a woman who could give him the one thing I could not—youth.

"Several of my friends have had similar experiences. Some refuse to consider divorce. They pretend not to see what is happening and hope the affair will blow over. I have too much pride for this. But what's the answer? How can a wife past forty hang on to her man when the competition is holding all the trump cards? Please tell me.

Defeated by Youth"

What "Defeated" refuses to admit is this: a man who finds fulfillment and contentment at home cannot be lured away by any woman—younger or older. I don't buy the theory that middle-aged men just naturally go for younger women. All men are attracted to women who are interesting and stimulating. A man is drawn to a woman who makes him feel virile and important. The wife may seem dreary and dull in contrast to the career woman. Or the wife may be so domineering and overpowering that her husband needs the reassurance of a less aggressive woman to restore his feeling of masculinity. The wife who is interesting and interested and who makes her husband feel more like a man than a cash register seldom has to worry about competition.

Women readers often ask if I know any secrets that will help them stay young. I do not. I have a few pet, unscientific tips, however, and here they are:

1. Don't let yourself get fat.

2. Keep your teeth in good repair.

3. If you *must* drink (and I am against it) keep the consumption down.

4. Don't select clothes that your granddaughter might wear. The fifty-two-year-old grandmother wearing a jumper and a Buster Brown hat doesn't look younger. She looks ridiculous and pitiable.

5. Go easy on the make-up after forty-five. A heavy foundation base and too much powder or rouge accentuate the wrinkles.

6. Know—and care about—what is happening in the world around you. A woman whose conversation is current and interesting is ageless.

If women would accept the fact that to be young is no achievement they would be more content. The real achievement is to make the best of every age as you live it. The woman who is forty-eight is exactly what she has made of herself. If she is a desirable woman, she is more attractive than she was at twenty-eight—and as young in spirit.

The men in our culture who can't accommodate to their years are equally pathetic. They are not always recognizable on sight in broad daylight—although some of the unfortunates can be found several hours a week in barber shops, trying everything from garlic cloves to sheep dip to save the fast-falling hair. The herd of aging buck are most active toward evening. They are the night prowlers—the latter-day Tom Cats who equate youth with virility.

Just being seen with a young girl massages their egos. One New York model wrote:

> "I can't figure Mr. M. out. He takes me to the finest places and spends money galore. This has been going on for five months. Although he is very affectionate when people are around, he has never made a serious pass. Incidentally, Mr. M. is about fifty-five and I am twenty-two. He has good connections in the dress business and I am a girl who wants to get ahead."

I told the girl I was happy she wanted to get ahead because she could certainly use one. I went on to explain that Mr. M. is interested only in a flattering ornament.

In almost every social group there is at least one male whose central conversational theme is sex. If the topic under discussion is politics, he has all the inside dope on the sex life of the candidates. If the conversation is foreign aid, he gets off on the sex habits of the natives. No matter what the subject, he is an absolute genius at using it as a bridge to get back to subject A. The person whose mind operates primarily along horizontal lines is sick—and more often than not, he is impotent. Conversation is his substitute for performance.

Youth should not be equated with virility. I receive many complaints from women married to men in their twenties who say their husbands have no interest in sex. And an even greater number of letters come from women in their sixties who complain of exhaustion because of their husbands' sexual demands.

The two letters which follow illustrate contrasting viewpoints. The first is from Greensboro, North Carolina:

"I'm a woman who is twenty-eight years old and the mother of two children. My husband is twenty-eight, also, and we have been married for six years. He treats me very nicely, we have no financial problems. He doesn't drink or gamble or pay attention to other women. In fact my problem is he doesn't even pay any attention to me. The last time he made love to me was on my birthday in February. (It was his birthday present.) I'm writing this letter, as you can see, on May 10. Please don't suggest that I tell him to go to the doctor. He has a physical check-up every year and is in excellent health. He is normal in every way and we get along together fine. I've mentiond this to him a few times and he says some people are interested in sex, and others are not—and he happens to be one who is not. What shall I do? I am."

From St. Petersburg, Florida:

"I am a woman in my early sixties. My husband is sixty-five. We have four children and fourteen lovely grandchildren. When we go out for an evening with friends, my husband gives me affectionate pats and caresses, which I don't mind too much, but when we get home he wants to keep it up. I've told him that people our age should be over that kind of foolishness. He says I am wrong. In fact he bragged that his grandfather married a thirty-three-year-old woman when he was seventy (second marriage) and they had two children. I can see that the nonsense is still running in his family. Please answer me in a plain envelope and tell me if this is respectable. I hope you say no." (She signed her letter, "Wish He'd Retire.")

I told the Greensboro woman that a twenty-eight-year-old man who bestows his "favors" once a year and calls it a birthday present has a clinker in his thinker and that he needs more than a physical check-up. He needs a mental check-up.

The St. Petersburg wife who "Wished He'd Retire" was told that sex activity between married people is respectable at any age. I added that she should be flattered. A good many men in their sixties enjoy pinching women other than their wives.

Youth is a state of mind. It is enthusiasm for life (or our lack of it) that pins the label of age on us. A keen mind can do more to make a woman's eyes sparkle than the most skillfully applied make-up. And I have yet to meet a man or woman who did not look years younger when smiling. A head held high, shoulders back, a brisk gait can knock off ten years and it costs nothing.

I once heard a doctor say, "You know, some people die in the very best of health." When I asked for an explanation, he said:

"It is easy to die when you have nothing to live for. In my practice I see patients who have a long list of organic defects, but they go on living actively and usefully in spite of their physical problems. I see other patients who die from relatively minor illnesses. I believe it is mainly because the fight has gone out of their lives. They die because they have no desire to go on living."

We all have known people who, in the evening of their lives, seemed hale and hearty, almost indestructible. Then, suddenly, the loss of a husband or a wife changed everything. The phrase, "He died of a broken heart" when translated into medical terms means, "His life no longer had meaning. It was easier to die than to live." Every doctor has had at least a few cases where the reverse was true. I have heard doctors say, "I would not have given him a chance for survival, but he simply refused to die."

The real trick is to stay alive as long as you live. To enjoy the blessings and the beauties that surround you and to make others glad that you are around. The key is to be active and useful and interested. This is the secret of staying alive as long as you live.

Some of the youngest people I know will never see seventy again. They are young because they have a lively enthusiasm for what is coming next. They are too fascinated with plans for the future to dwell in the past. They find life an exciting game because they are participants, not spectators. They are interesting people because they are interested people.

You are as young as your faith, as old as your doubt, as young as your courage, as old as your fear, as young as your dreams, as old as your despair. Walter Huston put it so well—"Age—it's only a number, Baby."

SEVENTEEN

Are you for real?

"May the outward and inward man be one."
Socrates

I GREW up in an atmosphere electric with Yiddish adages. My father was a sort of Jewish Lin Yutang. My mother had a talent for fitting an appropriate expression to any set of circumstances.

One of her favorites (and perhaps the one which first stimulated me to think beyond the literal meaning of words) was "Zie a mench." In English it means "Be a person." Since everyone is a person I reasoned that "Zie a mench" had to mean something more. So I asked. "A mench," explained my mother, "is a real person."

A real person is one who manages to be himself. This sounds elementary, and perhaps even naive, but don't be fooled. Being yourself is a challenging task because to be yourself you must know yourself. And few people do.

What are you really like? Would you be offended if I were to suggest that you are two people? Well, everyone is. ⟨First⟩ you are the self with the unattractive qualities—the secret desires, the large and small fears, the nagging insecurities, the twinges of envy and cowardice and avarice. ⟨Second⟩ is the self you proudly present to the world—courageous, confident, mature, selfless. This is the self each of us wants the world to see.

It is impossible to be 100 per cent for real. The society we live in requires that we behave in a prescribed manner, even though it may be contrary to our desires. But the better adjusted we are, the more real we are.

We have all encountered the phony with the false front. He talks big and does little. He is the eternal windbag, preaching one thing and practicing another—unreliable and unpredictable because no code of ethics governs his behavior. He folds in the clutch but is never without an airtight, water-proof alibi. Not only is his spine made of macaroni, but when his ego is punctured and the mask falls, another less attractive face is exposed.

The real person has a consistency which runs through every phase of his interpersonal relationships. He doesn't shower you with attention one day and ignore you the next. He doesn't wear one face for the company executives and another face for the company janitor. He doesn't smile sweetly to his dinner partner and then, within seconds, bark orders to the waiter. He has a quality of consistency which bespeaks reliability, dependability—and loyalty. He operates at a high ethical level and within a predictable framework. His responses to trying situations are disciplined and civilized. He doesn't switch positions, abandon his principles, or change his personality to fit his mood, the company, the weather, or the state of his digestion.

It's interesting to listen to a friend when he turns from

you to take a telephone call. Does his voice change? Or is it the same voice he used when he was talking to you? The real person is relaxed and he relaxes others. The phony is strained because he's working so hard at playing a role. It's exhausting to be on stage constantly, pretending and play-acting, never quite sure how the performance is coming off.

The real person uses a simple conversational alphabet. There is no capital "I," no small "u." He is not driven to exaggerate his virtues or his achievements. He doesn't pretend to be wealthier, wiser, better (or worse) behaved than he really is. He doesn't try to overwhelm others by name-dropping or place-dropping. The man who brags about his family tree betrays the fact that he is the sap. And we all know people who select their church, politics, and clubs solely on the basis of what the affiliation might do for them socially or financially.

Every organization has its bootlickers or at least one man with a gray flannel mouth. He goes through life with a moistened finger to the wind, never taking a stand until he is certain it's "safe." Conformity seems to assure security and respectability. Often, much of the real self is sacrificed in the process of fitting into the mold of what we think is expected of us.

It is becoming increasingly difficult in our society to be a real person because phoniness is built into our daily lives. Advertisements tell us that everything must look good, taste good, and smell good. If it doesn't, "scientists" are put to work to "improve" the product. We have become so enthralled with the ideal of youth and beauty that there are no limits some women won't test in giving nature a hand. They can display pearly white dentures, contact lenses, false eye-lashes, penciled brows, a surgically lifted face, plastic fingernails, tinted hair, a padded bra and derriere, too, if you please. Males have recourse to surgical face-lifting, too, and many go in for tinted hair, monkey-glands, and elevator shoes. There are advertisements for false hair which can be glued to the chest of a man who wishes to look virile in bathing trunks. (It is guaranteed not to come off in the water.)

A society which accepts so much external fakery is vulnerable to spiritual fraud as well. One of the prime ingredients of a real person is integrity. Diogenes would have to look even harder and longer today to find an honest man because the commercial rat race often offers the prize to the one who is willing to grab the quick but dishonest advantage. It takes strength to stick to principles in a world where the curve ball artists seem to be doing so well. Prosperity has grown a fatty tissue around our conscience. We are suffering from spiritual leukemia in a push-button, fur-lined age.

Personal integrity cannot be imposed by law. Laws have loopholes through which many a slippery character can crawl. We can act within the law and still be morally wrong. The true measure of the man is the level at which he operates when there are moral choices to be made.

What makes some people straight and others kinky? It is mostly a matter of early training, the major part of which is example. Those parents whose answers are evasive teach their youngsters the art of dancing around the truth. The small child who is lied to will lie to others. The mother who helps her teen-ager lie to Dad because "if he knew the truth he'd be furious" does the teen-ager no favor. Parents who choose the high road even though the low road seems the more advantageous, give their children an indispensable tool for building a good life.

A child who is brought up to respect truth has an enormous advantage. Integrity and a feeling of personal worth are assets more precious than an exceptional mind, good looks, or a winning personality. The so-called old-fashioned virtues are interdependent and where you find one you usually find others. People who participate in phony deals and shoddy business practices can usually be counted on to betray a friend. And the hackneyed adage that "blood is thicker than water" may be accurate chemically but that's as far as it goes. Every batch of my mail contains letters from readers who are suffering at the hands of relatives. Business deals in which brother cheats brother, inheritance wrangles where one or two members of a family bilk a widow or the surviving children are every day occurrences. None of us can safely assume that a relative can be trusted merely because he is a relative. The real person who has decent principles and high moral standards will treat all people fairly. The unprincipled character will take anybody he can—relatives included.

The opening paragraphs of this chapter suggest that no one is 100 per cent for real. Why? Because society won't permit it. The twentieth century two-legged animal is expected to be tactful. Civilized behavior demands that we sublimate minor hostilities and frustrations in order to get along with others. In dozens of small ways man accommodates. He must compromise with absolute truth if he is mature enough to place a higher value on the feelings of others than on his own comfort or convenience. Every man must set his personal limits, however. He must decide the point at which he will refuse to allow inconsiderate people to take advantage of him. Too often, a cruel or unthinking person will club his victim over the head with "the truth" and call it "friendship."

It is the central business of every human being to work toward being as real as it is within his power to be. Psychiatrists tell us that the healthy personality is whole—it is all of a piece. This means the individual has resolved the major conflicts within himself and he is not compelled to act one way and feel another.

William James described this struggle as "zerrissenheit" which means "torn to pieces-ness." There are times in our lives when feelings of defeat or fear make us feel that our world is falling apart and the temptation is to fall apart with it. The real person refuses to give way to "zerrissenheit." He keeps himself together. He accepts himself with his limitations and his imperfections—without shame or sham. He can tolerate frustration or defeat. He can regroup and rebuild. He is kept afloat by the knowledge that he has what it takes to recover and try again. An unmistakable hallmark of realness is the ability to meet all situations with dignity and maturity.

If you can truthfully say that you are on good terms with yourself, if the image you project to others bears a family resemblance to the kind of person you believe you are, if you say what you mean and mean what you say, and if you are willing to admit that there is just a little bit of the phony in you—you are for real.